THE CONFLICT RESOLUTION CURRICULUM FOR CHILDREN IN EMOTIONAL CONFLICT

With Objectives, Activities, and Evaluations for IEP's

By

MICHAEL R. SELF, Ed.D.

University of Alabama
Huntsville, Alabama

CHARLES   C   THOMAS   •   PUBLISHER
Springfield • Illinois • U.S.A.

Published and Distributed Throughout the World by

CHARLES C THOMAS • PUBLISHER

2600 South First Street

Springfield, Illinois, 62717, U.S.A.

© *1982 by* CHARLES C THOMAS • PUBLISHER

ISBN 0-398-04596-8

·Library of Congress Catalog Card Number: 81-14491

Printed in the United States of America
CU-RX-1

Library of Congress Cataloging in Publication Data

Self, Michael R.
   The conflict resolution curriculum for children in
emotional conflict.

   Bibliography: p.
   Includes index.
   1. Child psychotherapy.   2. Mentally ill children--
Education.   I. Title.   [DNLM: 1. Affective symptoms--
In infancy and childhood.   2. Conflict (Psychology)--In
infancy and childhood.   3. Affective symptoms--Therapy.
4. Curriculum.   WS 350.6 S465c]
RJ504.2.S44   618.92'8914   81-14491
ISBN 0-398-04596-8   AACR2

THE CONFLICT RESOLUTION CURRICULUM FOR CHILDREN IN EMOTIONAL CONFLICT

PREFACE

WRITING a how-to book for use in working with children with emotional problems is a very ambitious and presumptuous endeavor. Ambitious in that with countless volumes of books and journals already filled with information (factual and conjecture) about theory, causation, identification, etiology, prognosis, intervention, environment, family, and motivation of children with emotional problems, what more could or should be added? Ambitious, too, in its effort to simplify some of those voluminous writings and tie much of that information into a succinct framework for effective intervention with children. And finally, ambitious in its attempt to put on paper some of the ideas, techniques, and experiences that contribute to the development of that elusive quality that distinguishes the better interventioners from the so-so ones.

This book is presumptuous in that what is written on the following pages hopefully won't be a waste of the reader's time to read, since most of the writing is the author's interpretation of the previously alluded to information, tempered by experience and time. It is presumptuous, too, in that the ideas and techniques advocated herein can work for others as they have worked in the past. The techniques and procedures depicted represent one approach, not necessarily "the" approach or the only approach, but one approach that has proven very effective over time. If this book or one little idea contained within it reaffirms the correctness of the reader's own approach to him/herself, or if the book helps one person intervene successfully with one child in need, then the effort and pain endured to write it will have been worth the trouble.

M.R.S.

ACKNOWLEDGMENTS

W HILE this may be the least read page in the entire book, it allows me the opportunity to publicly acknowledge and thank those persons that contributed to my bringing this effort to fruition. My basic acknowledgment would have to be to all the children in conflict with whom I have worked over the years and who have taught me so much. They tested, pushed, challenged, and molded my thinking.

I also must thank the various teachers-in-training that were gracious enough to be sounding boards for my ideas and thoughts regarding the actual curriculum. Foremost among those would be Ron Glass, Patsy Johnson, and Betty Wagner. Thanks too to my mentor, Dr. Ludrick Linkous, for just being my mentor.

The actual manuscript preparation was presided over by many people. So, again, I say thanks to Barbara Menzie for editing the original draft and to all the typists, Mary Hunt and Sharon Jean at UCLA and Alfreda Smith, Anne Schoenknecht, and Doreen Fulcher at The University of Alabama in Huntsville.

Michael Self

CONTENTS

THE CONFLICT
RESOLUTION CURRICULUM
FOR CHILDREN IN
EMOTIONAL CONFLICT

CHAPTER 1

STATE OF THE ART

ONE of the reasons for putting ideas into print is to facilitate communication. Through communication comes a sharing of ideas, questioning, agreement, disagreement, new directions, and with luck, growth. As with many texts on behavior disorders, this one begins with a look at the traditional historical development of the field. I have attempted to address the significant events and issues in behavior disorders. My overall assessment constitutes a state-of-the-art review. One of the reasons for doing this is to get readers immediately involved in thinking and deciding for themselves where they stand on the events and issues discussed herein.

Three domains will be explored to review the area of *children in conflict* (term from Reinert, 1976). First, what have been the significant events relative to children in conflict in the recent past? Second, what are the significant issues? And third, has anything significantly new been contributed?

RECENT MAJOR EVENTS IN BEHAVIOR DISORDERS

At least four major events have occurred in recent years that have had a significant impact on services provided to children in conflict. The first involves societal circumstances. The yearly Gallup poll on education still shows that lack of discipline in the classroom is of utmost concern to parents who send their children to public schools. Classroom teachers consistently report spending more and more of their time attempting to achieve and maintain discipline with little time left for instruction. Inner-city ghettos are still producing street gangs, and more and more schools are becoming armed camps. Teachers are almost routinely being threatened, intimidated, assaulted, stabbed, and shot in the course of fulfilling their teaching duties. The recent Carneigie Study Group on Education (1979) has advocated a complete revamping of the "monolithic" high school, because it is not meeting the needs of a majority of its students. Although figures vary, conservatively 8-10 percent of school-aged children are in need of some degree of mental health intervention.

Single families are on the increase. Divorce affects two out of five families and is quickly approaching half of all families. Only 7 percent of all families in America have a parent that remains home full time exclusively to raise their children. Those families that do remain intact have been confronted with the necessity of both parents having to work to make financial ends meet. Eighty percent of all families earning over $20,000 yearly have both parents working.

The effect of this has been to throw traditional child-rearing practices into almost complete upheaval. Parents and guardians alike are confused, frustrated, and disheartened in attempting to impart values to their children. Ever-increasing numbers of children are left unsupervised for longer and longer periods of time at earlier and earlier ages. More children are missing critical structuring and guidance during the two-to-five year age span. Increasing numbers of children go to school completely unprepared to learn. "Enlightened" parents have not encouraged self-discipline in their children and contribute unknowingly to a traumatic transition for their child when he/she arrives at school for the first time. Teachers, themselves, have become victims and perpetrators of a system that does not have time for individual differences. Teachers have long been thought of as "socializing agents" to teach the child all the skills he should have learned at home. The final result is that ever-increasing numbers of students are being identified by their parents, teachers, and administrators as having emotional problems.

A second major event to affect services to children in conflict has been the introduction and wholesale adoption of learning theory techniques to education. The techniques, themselves, are generally referred to as behavior modification or more colloquially as "B-Mod." The sheer magnitude of their use easily qualifies them as an event. Fifteen years of concerted use has given ample opportunity for certain conclusions to be drawn about the positive and negative aspects of behavior modification. On the positive side, it appears that anyone can be taught the basic principles and techniques for applications. This would include teachers, parents, administrators, aides, bus drivers, peers, etc. This fact makes their use economical in that highly trained professionals can spend more time in individual therapy while an aide or paraprofessional can maintain larger groups. The techniques are easy to master and are very effective when applied conscientiously by inexperienced practitioners. The techniques also provide structure and a consistent approach when working with problem children i.e. *structure* in that they describe how to implement and carry out a behavior change program, and *consistent* in that, if used judiciously, the techniques work from child to child and teacher to teacher similarly. Possibly the greatest asset of learning theory is its effectiveness with severely handicapped children, regardless of exceptionality. For years many people felt that little if anything could be accomplished by working with severe and profound exceptionalities. Learning theorists have ably demonstrated that severe and profound clients can acquire varying degrees of language skills, motor skills, social skills, and cognitive skills if a client's individual program can provide adequate or minute sequential steps that are repetitious and amply reinforced.

On the negative side, certain drawbacks do remain. The biggest and most persistent problem is the frequent lack of generalization of a client's newfound behavior from a reinforcing situation to a nonreinforcing situation. The following true situation underscores the problem. A client in an institution for the mentally retarded exhibited an inordinate amount of head-banging behavior.

The teacher for the educational component of his program developed and successfully implemented a behavior modification program to reward ever-increasing periods of non-head-banging. At the culmination of the program the child exhibited no head-banging behavior in the classroom. However, upon returning to his ward where he was one of sixty clients tended by one therapist, the head-banging returned. The client was either discriminating what would get him noticed (reinforcement) in each setting or was not generalizing the skills apparently acquired in one setting to another setting. The learning theorist is quick to reply to this tale that (1) the behavior was not sufficiently reinforced in the former setting to allow it to be sufficiently maintained in the nonreinforcing setting, or (2) someone on the ward should have been informed of the program to maintain the new behavior on the ward. Either argument is very valid, but neither addresses the real issue. The non-head-banging behavior was not internalized by the client. Internalization is a concept not recognized in the strictest sense by a learning theory purist, because it deals with internal feelings and not environmental contingencies or external shapers of behavior. The client did not internalize the need not to bang his head, but was merely conditioned not to bang his head to achieve his reward for not doing so.

This problem raises another negative aspect: the more astute problem child can consciously recognize a reward or "payoff" for good or appropriate behavior; therefore, he is able to control his behavior to achieve his desired reward. On the face value of this, the teacher is happy because the child's behavior is appropriate or at least non-destructive. However, when the child leaves the room and moves to another teacher, he is still disruptive. What has happened is that the child has learned a very valuable lesson on how to play the "game." The child is manipulating his environment to get what he, and not the teacher, wants. The teacher wants adaptive behaviors, but is settling for mere control, while the child is learning to "con" the teacher to get his payoff. A moral question exists here that has to be resolved not in a textbook, but rather by each individual confronted with this dilemma.

A third area of concern in the application of behavior modification is the gradual evolvement of its use by teachers into an ever-increasing emphasis on the negative. Said more plainly, perhaps B-Mod is used more and more for punishment and not so much for shaping behavior positively. From the child's perspective, behavior is not changed through positive rewarding so much as it is through fear of the consequences for not doing something appropriately. A clearer understanding of this point might be achieved if one reflects on the natural occurrence of events in a typical classroom that employs B-Mod techniques. The goal ostensibly is to heap ample rewards on a child every time he exhibits the target behavior that is being shaped, and this is usually done in the beginning. Ever notice how hard it is to reward good behavior positively? If a child is doing what he is supposed to do, the teacher tends to overlook that child because he is only doing what is expected. Instead the teacher spends most of her energy with the more disruptive child. Eventually, contingencies are established between teacher and child. The contingencies go something like this: "If you misbehave, then I will punish you by taking away a privilege." It should be, "If you behave, I will reward you by letting you do something you like." Teachers do not initially intend to emphasize the negative aspect of behavior, but many do evolve into this stance primarily because it requires less effort to punish an event after it occurs, rather than expend a great deal of effort noticing and praising appropriate behavior to prevent its antithetic behavior. Alternatives to this predicament will be discussed in Chapter 3.

A final concern regarding B-Mod is its seemingly widespread unconscientious application by teachers. Teachers will frequently design programs for children without really anticipating the effects of their plan. For instance, you cannot plan to ignore physical aggression by a child if he/she stands to harm someone else, or you cannot ignore certain attention-seeking behaviors by children if they are being reinforced by peers and not the teacher. Too, it is not wise to attempt to exert peer pressure on a child by taking away everyone's ice cream at lunch because one or two children misbehaved. The use of "time-out" provides another example. By definition, *time-out* is removal from a positive environment, yet many teachers establish as a contingency the removal of a child from a classroom to time-out for misbehavior. Two abuses are evident: one, many teachers place children into time-out for relatively minor offenses, and two, the time-out is usually more rewarding to the child than the classroom. All of the above are illustrative of unconscientious use of B-Mod techniques. The reader would probably not be hard pressed to cite other examples.

A third significant event in the field of behavior disorders is recent, and the extent of its contributions to helping children in conflict is still not fully evident. Its effects have raised more questions perhaps than have been answered, but various aspects can be speculated upon with certainty. The event is the proliferation of what are commonly alluded to as modern therapies. The modern therapies include, but are not limited to, Transactional Analysis, Teacher (or Parent) Effectiveness Training, Transcedental Meditation, Reality Therapy, Rational Emotive Therapy, Primal Scream, Relaxation Therapy, Biofeedback, Assertiveness Training, Achievement Motivation, Wayne Dyer's philosophy (*Pulling Your Own Strings* (1979), *Your Erroneous Zones* (1977) etc.), EST, and EKANKAR. These approaches are very popular. Why and what are they really saying? They have either contributed to or are the result of the era of "Do your own thing" or the "me" generation. Resolution of the issue of causality is not germane to the fact that people today are very much into doing their own thing. Perhaps due to increased leisure time, more affluence, mass media, more education, or more recognition of mental health needs, more people are turning to the modern therapies for direction in leading more fulfilled lives. However stated, their collective intent is to aid people in breaking the emotional circle they find themselves in when confronted with recurring problems. Their goal is to help consumers accept the responsibility for leading their own lives fully, successfully, and independently, and to help the cause for adaptive behavior through increased coping skills.

What does it mean to do one's own thing? On the one negative side, it means to quit if things don't go your way, dropping out if the system is unchangeable, or simply going your own way regardless of the effect or consequences on yourself or others. On the other hand, it means becoming self-actualized, or doing what you really want to do, even if you're viewed as a nonconformist. Becoming self-actualized also means breaking old habits or patterns, which in turn also means not feeling guilty about doing so. A marvelous, easy-to-read book for making one feel not guilty about all the guilt trips people routinely experience about such issues as change, family ties, religion, sex, parenthood, divorce, money success, status, jobs, and traditions has been written by Paula and Dick McDonald (1977) entitled *Guilt Free*. Doing what is best for oneself and not feeling guilty about doing it is very difficult, and the modern therapies purport to show people how to achieve goals without being crippled by guilt for doing so.

There are at least two contributing factors to the search for self-actualization. The first is accurate but unsubstantiated by research, while the second has been frequently cited in contemporary literature. For want of a better title, the first is called the "Great Depression" condition. Briefly, it refers to children that grew up during the depression years of the early 1930s. Those children made a promise to themselves that when they grew up and had children of their own, their children would want for nothing and would not have to experience the desolution that their parents had been forced to endure. Additionally, family units were very close and interdependent upon each family member. Then during the post-World War II era, America entered an age of affluence. As the children of the thirties became the parents of the fifties, they began heaping material possessions on their children. Frequently these were unearned by the child and not connected to the development of any sense of responsibility: they were simply free. Large numbers of children began growing up expecting unearned rewards and seeking more material possessions. Every family on the block raced to be the first to get a TV, a dishwasher, blenders, two cars, three cars, power mowers, etc. Television brought the world into the living room, and cars scattered the now mobile family everywhere.

The children of the fifties have become the parents of the seventies and are into whatever is "in" at the time. They tell their children to try everything (it does not seem to matter if they finish it or not). They encourage their child to quit if he/she cannot be the star of the team, or head cheerleader, or first chair in the band, or captain of the school patrol, etc. The result, of course, is more children in school that cannot finish tasks, are not self-motivated or self-disciplined, and lack any concept of what constitutes structure.

The impersonal "system" is the second contributing factor to increased self-actualization via the modern therapies. As bureaucracies have become larger and more unresponsive, as big business has become more distant, as politicians become more inaccessible, as insurance and utility rates climb ever upward, the average person has somehow been lost in the shuffle. The result is apathy toward government involvement, resignation and acceptance of consumer fraud, higher absenteeism at school and work, poor workmanship, divorce, and the ultimate dropout, suicide. People look around them at what they see as the breakdown of the old system, the establishment, religion, and moral values. They ask themselves "who cares?" At this point they have two ways to go. They can either rip off the system, drop out, grab whatever they can for themselves and be nobody's fool, or choose not to be lost in the shuffle and seek to become the best possible person they can be through self-actualization. The intent here is not to paint a bleak picture, but rather to impress upon the reader that the increased numbers of children in conflict in our schools are the result of long developing social conditions that are as evident and yet as complex as each individual that makes up our society. There are no easy solutions.

What do the modern therapies offer over the traditional therapies of Freud, Watson, Erickson, Skinner, Durkheim, and others? Many would probably argue vehemently that the two are completely dissimilar. Yet it is not difficult to see the relationship of Berne's Transactional Analysis to psychoanalytical thinking, or Glasser's Reality Therapy to traditional psychodynamic tenets, or Achievement Motivation Training to learning theory. What then are the differences between modern and traditional therapies? The real differences have been the infusion of new language into the traditional jargon and the demystification of personal psychology, so that everyone can become a lay psychologist.

There are real issues, though, related to the use of the modern therapies. On the positive side, they have made great strides in simplifying the language of psychology. The therapies have taken more of a realistic, commonsense orientation to solve personal problems and have provided detailed mechanisms for helping people to break those old maladaptive behavioral patterns. Additionally, they foster increased self-confidence in one's ability to control one's own life, also known as personal independence. Central to the realization of this point has been the increased acceptance of individualization, or nonconformity, in today's society.

Negatively, the modern therapies have at least three major drawbacks. The first is the problem of transferred dependency. Many people simply cringe at having to make decisions. They prefer to let someone else take the responsibility for that. Once a decision has been reached, they are eager to help implement it. Thus, a person unable to stand on his own to make decisions will seek group therapies or individual counseling or go from counselor to counselor looking for the answers to their problems, never really accepting the obvious: we have to stand alone and make our own decisions after first having gathered as much information as is needed from whatever source to make those decisions. Many people do not know when to quit therapy because they have no goal in mind when they start, so they have no clear idea of when they reach it; hence, increased transferred dependency. Second, if everyone is doing their own thing as advocated by many of the therapies, are they really cognizant of the need for self-discipline? How do we teach problem children to restrain themselves if the significant others around them cannot even achieve token self-discipline. This is a serious matter that requires conscientious efforts to redress. The third drawback evolves from the axiom of modern therapies that encourages people to say what is on their minds; to be verbally honest and straightforward about one's feelings toward things or people. There exists a thin line between being verbally assertive and downright aggressive (which connotes hostility). In using the modern therapies, restraints should be incorporated that attack these problems and still allow the person to benefit by the therapies.

Can these approaches be applied to the classroom? More specifically, will they work with a classroom of children experiencing emotional conflicts? In actuality they have been used to varying degrees in special education classes for behaviorally disturbed students. Though conservatively used, they have met with generally positive results. While all the therapies listed earlier have had some application, the approaches that have probably seen the greatest use are Reality Therapy (Glasser, 1965), Transactional Analysis (Berne, 1967), and Achievement Motivation. As with everything else, their use has raised still more questions. Of concern here is the effect these multitherapies will or have had on the attainment of a unification model of intervention for children in conflict.

The very fact that there are so many different therapies in use is another indication of the state of the art in behavior disorders. There simply is no widely accepted single theory that offers answers to every question that might arise on how best to achieve adaptive behavior with problem children. As Rhodes and Tracy (1972) pointed out in their conceptual project in emotional disturbance, the various proffered theories of causality and intervention are really only incomplete models. Rhodes's own ecological model most closely approximates a complete unification theory, and probably the only reason it has not been embraced more widely is the reluctance of the subscribers of the other models to relinquish their adamant positions. A lesser reason is a little more deceptive. The strongest arguers for any given position are typically the ones furthest away from providing direct services to problem children, i.e. academicians, while those on the front line of service provision, and who tend to be the most successful are more eclectic. Being eclectic is also a deterrent to recognizing one unified approach. If one is eclectic, one does not have to label one's approach; it is just eclectic. Many equate an eclectic approach with a "green-thumb" approach: whatever works, use it. This is unfortunate. The consumer of a green-thumb approach does not really examine the interrelatedness of his actions, whereas a unified approach like Rhodes's explains how changes in overt behavior will influence one's feelings about one's self-image. Too, the truly well thought out eclectic theories of the recent past go by different names, which only hinder the recognition of one truly unified approach to working with children in conflict.

Will the modern therapies then help or hinder a unification theory? This question cannot be answered directly. There is a great deal of similarity in all the approaches, only the packaging is different in many cases. The real hinderance of the various modern therapies is that they tend to reinforce in everyone sooner or later that their own unique approach or classroom program coincides with this or that particular therapy and therefore must be OK. This indirect reinforcement must surely reinforce one's resistance to change and, hence, adversely affect movement toward a unification theory of intervention. One positive effect of the modern therapies is that almost anyone can be instructed in their use and application, and as more people become proficient in their use, more people are going to become aware of the need for mental health services, and this will aid tremendously in carrying us toward improved coping skills and more adaptive behavior. A final problem with the modern therapies is that many of them have been popularized on the personal charisma of their particular founder. Enough is known about the relationship between the success of various innovative projects and ideas and their founder's or director's personal charisma, to say that frequently when the charismatic personality leaves, much is lost from the original idea or program, so much that in some cases the program or philosophy dies. Again, this frequently manifests itself during replication. One therapist may be very good at applying Reality Therapy (Glasser, 1965), for example, to a classroom of behaviorally disordered children; yet, if someone else tries to replicate, they may fail miserably, because the personality factor of the therapist cannot be accounted for completely in any of the modern therapies.

The fourth and final event has been the recent, renewed emphasis on providing public school services to children in emotional conflict (EC). This renewed interest is obviously a result of local education agencies (LEA) efforts to implement PL 94-142. Prior to the passage of PL 94-142, EC children like many other children of various other exceptionalities were routinely denied equal access to least restrictive environments (LRE) and mainstreaming opportunities. Much of the services provided EC children prior to PL 94-142 was provided in residential facilities, university-related clinics, funded projects, training labs, state institutions for the mentally ill, hospitals, and local or regional mental health facilities. In proportion to the numbers of classes for the retarded and learning disabled in public school systems, the number of EC classes has traditionally been very small. This is true not because there were not enough EC children but rather because they were not being identified as a result of the reluctance of administrators in wanting to explain to parents that their child was emotionally disturbed. Of all the exceptionalities, more parents take the emotionally disturbed label as a personal affront to their abilities to parent and typically experience inordinate amounts of guilt. This guilt usually manifests itself as anger toward the school system, hence the school system's hesitation to bring this on themselves. Instead of attempting to work with these parents, the LEAs have chosen to persuade themselves that they have no emotionally disturbed children in their system.

An additional facet of this seeming reluctance to provide services becomes clearer if one recognizes that at the time PL 94-142 was passed, most LEAs and many state education agencies (SEA) had no succinct plan to implement services to children in conflict. Thus, in response to the PL 94-142 mandate, many LEAs simply rushed in completely unprepared to provide realistic services. What has resulted in many systems is a very disparate range of services, serving a likewise wide range of children in an often incoherent fashion, which indirectly supports an earlier statement that, as a field, behavior disorders still lacks a unified theoretical and philosophical approach. The problem was compounded by a lack of sufficient numbers of qualified teachers to work with the children already identified as being children in conflict. Training institutions generally respond to the law of supply and demand. By this is meant that if a state is not hiring teachers to work with EC children (because they have no EC program), then the institutions are not going to be training teachers. Also, when the SEA finally decides to provide services, it takes at least two years for institutions to respond with increased numbers of teachers. With today's tight economy, future teachers are going to invest their money in an area where the future job market is expected. Thus, LEAs are frequently forced into hiring an untrained teacher or one who agrees to go back to school in a new area and become a "retread." Herein are added further problems. Local Education Agencies are hiring teachers without proper training, but who are willing to go back to school to get that training, and, additionally, who have seldom seen or worked with problem children. Also, with teaching jobs becoming more scarce in regular education, droves of preservice teachers are migrating to special education, not because they are particularly interested in exceptional children but rather because this is where the jobs are. Either way there is not enough quality control being exercised over the kind of teacher that school systems are letting work with behaviorally troubled children. Many teachers have problems of their own that do not need to be laid on a child with his own unique needs. Once the teacher is in the classroom, it is too late to discover that he/she cannot cope with the students. This may be one reason behind the fact that during the mid-1970s the average classroom tenure or length of stay of all special education teachers was only eighteen months.

Faced with the mandate to serve EC children, the LEAs typically took one of at least five options afforded them:

1. Many contracted with local mental health agencies to provide services. In some instances the services have been very good, but as always there were problems with this approach. Whenever two autonomous agencies endeavor to work together cooperatively toward a common goal, certain frictions are inevitable. The two most commonly occurring frictions were *money* and *outside control*. Because mental health agencies need to be as self-supporting as possible, they are expensive, and with EC children frequently needing very low therapist-to-client ratios, mental health services become even more expensive. Also, education agencies frequently report a sense of helplessness in exerting control over the direction of the services provided by mental health agencies. These two factors combined have resulted in a general trend away from contracting with mental health agencies for services to EC children.

2. Another option exercised by some LEAs has been to hire someone outside the educational field to come in and establish EC services in the system. Oftentimes, this person has been a psychologist or counselor and frequently has had mental health experience. When this approach has not worked, it is usually due to the lack of transition of the person from the outside-of-education system to the education system. Psychologists are accustomed to hourly sessions with clients and not to scheduling a child through an entire day with all the support the child might need. This can be a difficult transition to make. Learning to work with teachers is always a tough task, and many psychologists have approached teachers with condescension, which automatically sabotages any efforts by the psychologist to implement services.

3. A third option being used more and more, fortunately, is to hire a certified EC teacher to establish a program. Working under the direction of a special education coordinator, these properly trained individuals are making slow but sure progress toward quality programs. This is the preferred course because it keeps all services within the domain of the LEA, allows for full-time services, and is seen as a school-related service rather than as a tacked-on appendage.

4. When LEAs have sought to set up internally run programs but have been unable to secure competently trained personnel, they have exercised a fourth option. This option has been to hire an untrained teacher willing to get properly credentialed and also to hire outside consultants to help get the program going. Many times the consultant is a professor from a regional teacher training institution. This approach works in proportion to the experience and personality of the consultant hired. If the consultant has had recent experiences with EC children, then he usually can succeed in helping to establish a viable program. Many successful programs have been initiated in this fashion. The only real drawbacks to this approach

are that sometimes a consultant is hired who may have established a good reputation for himself years ago, but has not seen or worked with problem children in a long time, which in turn affects the practicality and reality of his suggestions. The most acute drawback is that such consultants simply are not there enough. Invariably when they are needed the most (as in a crisis), they are not there.

5. The final option, which is really no option at all, is to have no program whatsoever. It is still surprising how many school systems have taken this option!

An equally important aspect of the effect of PL 94-142 on improved services for EC students has been the increased attention to, and services for, the more severely emotionally conflicted child. How are systems providing for children with severe problems? It is clear that more and more EC cases are showing up in public schools. Although it is too early to assess the effects of this trend critically, certain observations can be made:

1. How realistic and appropriate is it to serve EC children in public schools? With the recent trend toward decentralization of state mental institutions, with ever-shrinking mental health dollars, and with the PL 94-142 mandate, there has been a concerted effort for public schools to provide for the severely EC child. Yet, are schools equipped to handle this child? Are LEAs adequately prepared to spend the money to house these students, and are they prepared for the potential destructiveness and possible harm done if a child violently explodes?

2. Not just anyone can walk into a class of severely EC children and carry out a successful intervention program. It truly takes a special teacher to handle violent behavior, self-mutilation, spit, soiled pants, complete unattentiveness, and very, very slow, if indeed any, progress. And all this day after day after day after day. An inordinate amount of patience is an automatic prerequisite, but it takes a differently trained individual to work with severely EC children. It takes someone thoroughly trained in learning theory, behavioral analysis, task analysis, criterion-referenced teaching, data collection, record keeping, and home monitoring, but most of all it takes experience.

3. The cost-to-benefit ratio is going to have to be carefully scrutinized. Remodeling rooms, building new observation rooms and time-out rooms, buying special buses and getting the bus drivers, aides, and teachers for one-on-one intervention for six children is very expensive, and no one has to be told how fierce the competition for education dollars is and how pressed school boards are for maximum accountability of every school dollar spent. And in the end, what is this going to buy: high-priced baby-sitting, or real gains?

4. As the competing dollars are being spent to meet the requirements of PL

94-142 there are going to be less dollars remaining to serve the mildly and moderately EC child. They are going to be left in the mainstream, all right but completely unserviced. Who stands to gain the most from those intervention dollars, and who stands the greater likelihood of contributing to society by not burdening it? These are very real and agonizing considerations that face today's LEAs and merit much closer examination by *everyone* involved.

CURRENT ISSUES IN BEHAVIOR DISORDERS

In the context of their use here, *issues* differ from *events* in that events reflect single occurrences or significant influences on the direction in which a field moves. Events in and of themselves may have decided effects on issues. Issues meanwhile are ongoing, unresolved, heatedly discussed problems where all sides know they are right, and involve matters generally at the core of the field. The following issues are certainly not all-inclusive but do hopefully reflect some of the major issues concerning the provision of services to EC children.

The first issue is *terminology*. What do we call these children? The current state of affairs is reflected in the numerous terms used thus far in the present text to describe the same child. Is the appropriate term *emotionally disturbed, behaviorally disordered, emotionally conflicted*, or *children in conflict*? The answer depends on your training and philosophical perspective.

If you believe that a child's emotional problems respond best to therapy when treated as a disease or as a separate entity, then you are a subscriber to the medical model, and the appropriate term for you to use is emotionally disturbed (ED). The medical model denotes the general approach taken by physicians and psychiatrists in working with illness. They are trained to envision the host body being invaded by some disease or entity, and their task is to "cure" the individual. This has been the predominant approach of most mental health programs in helping the mentally ill or ED client. When education started providing for problem children, mental health professionals were the only professionals available with the appropriate knowledge and experience. Thus, when they began migrating to education, they brought their terminology with them. Their "cure" was either psychotherapy or drugs. Their goal then was to heal the afflicted child of his illness. There was just one slight problem. The connotation that the ED term provoked in the minds of parents of ED children caused a very strong, negative reaction. The ED term arouses a great deal of guilt in most parents, guilt from the feeling that they have failed as parents. This guilt is associated with the fact that our society is very child oriented. Parents expend vast amounts of time, energy, and money raising "perfect" reflections of themselves and are crushed if their child is a failure! Parents somehow see the failure as their own and not the child's. This arouses guilt and embarrassment that their friends might notice. Whether rational and justified or not, this is the frequent reaction of parents when told their child is ED. Their subconscious guilt manifests itself as exaggerated anger, and most school boards and administrators do not want angry parents.

An alternative term used to replace ED was *behavior disorders* (BD). This term went a long way toward divorcing education from the mental health field and alleviated a lot of the guilt experienced by parents, so that schools could at least begin to get children into appropriate kinds of services for a child's emotional problems. Although no hard data are cited, a general observation would be that half the literature uses ED, while the other half will use BD. Other terms are used but not with enough regularity to be considered as serious contenders or substitutes for the ED or BD nomenclature. A further distinction is offered by Hewett (1980). He points out that the term, "emotional disturbance," is vague and not directly identifiable, whereas the term, "behavior disorders," denotes problems in behavior that are identifiable.

But problems still exist with the BD label. To many, it still implies that the problem resides within the individual, when in fact the problem may be in the environment (Reinert, 1976). Another problem with the ED-BD terminology is the ease with which unaffected individuals can dissociate emphatically from problem children. When people dissociate themselves from others' problems, they also divest themselves of the responsibility of helping those people. Reinert (1976) presented a possible alternative with his term, *children in conflict*. His concept can be expanded further, however.

In Alabama, the term *emotional conflict* (EC) is used in reference to children in conflict. Reinert correctly uses the term, "children in conflict," to make his point that emotional problems are not always something that reside within the individual, but can be caused and maintained by the environment. Dr. Ludrick Linkous, who was the driving force behind Alabama's adoption of the term, "EC," had previously expanded on the point Reinert stresses to point out that all people experience emotional conflicts.* Granted, some people experience them to a greater or lesser degree than do others, but we all have conflicts. They may be internal (as when a decision between right and wrong must be made), or they may be between two individuals (as when spouses disagree), or they may be between the individual and his environment (as when we don't make enough money to pay our bills). The fact still remains that we all have conflicts, and as such, we need to be more cognizant of the emotional needs of those less fortunate than ourselves. It has even been hypothesized that unless we experience and successfully resolve our personal conflicts, we cease to grow as emotional individuals. This is supported by the notion that when we have no problems, we tend to become complacent. Henceforth, in this text, whenever possible, the term, "EC," will be used to refer to all problem children.

The next issue is a broad and mixed one but ultimately an issue of definition. As discussed previously, it is the issue of what to call these obviously

---

*Linkous, Ludrick 1974: personal communication.

troubled children. A compromise to the traditional hard and fast labels of ED-BD was offered in the term "EC." Now that these children have been tentatively labeled, they need to be studied, and to study them they need to be defined, either as a group or individually. Yet, when the literature is perused, a single, universally accepted definition is not found, but rather a multitude of sometimes inadequate and seemingly conflicting definitions.

One of the better discussions relative to this issue is to be found in Kauffman (1977, pp. 14-23). The reader is referred to this text for a more thorough discussion than will be rendered here; however, Kauffman will be cited to examine two specific aspects. The first deals with the various definitions of EC, while the second concerns the reasons behind the lack of a single universally accepted definition. The different definitions are reflective of the particular orientation and training emphasis of the given fields from whence the definitions originate. For instance, from a psychodynamic viewpoint *conflict* is viewed as internal strife, needing insight to understand and hence to resolve, while learning theory espouses a concept of conflict that is initiated and maintained by the environment, completely external to the individual's feelings. The problems caused by these numerous definitions add to the confusion in an already confused field.

For instance, if you were the parent of a child in conflict and heard the two previously mentioned concepts of conflict, and their resultant intervention strategies, that are likewise different? which would you believe and ultimately follow? Many parents of conflicted children are routinely confronted with this dilemma. These same definitions cause their respective proponents to look at the same child with the same presenting behaviors in entirely different ways. The effect of this assessment perspective has been to encourage the professional to make the child fit his/her idea or concept of conflict, whether in actuality the child does or does not. This is a grievous error. Again, for emphasis, it causes us to make that child fit *our* concept of conflict, instead of examining the child where he/she really exists to come up with a fair and accurate diagnosis. Additionally, when one restricts oneself to a single esoteric viewpoint, there is an increased probability that the person will "miss" something that another viewpoint could very possibly have added. For example, if one is looking for internally caused conflict, he or she might miss an external event that is significantly adding to the problem. Listed here are composite interpretations of some of the more widely used definitions of conflict (Haring, 1978; Kauffman, 1977; Reinert, 1976; Rhodes and Tracy, 1972).

A *psychoanalytic* definition would explain conflict as initiating in childhood. It is during childhood that a child would have fixated during one of the psychosexual stages. His/Her inability to successfully develop the insight necessary to resolve these earlier, deep-seated conflicts would interfere with his/her ability to handle present-day problems. This person has a weak ego function.

A *psychodynamic* definition would also contribute one's problems to internal conflicts. The problem may have originated when the individual did not successfully navigate the various psychosocial (Erikson, 1963) stages of his/her youth, but is dealt with in terms of the person's inability to cope with their present-day problems.

The proponents of a *biological etiology of conflict* point to organic causes of disturbance. The person may have a genetic disorder, a metabolic imbalance, a mineral deficiency, or irregular brain waves contributing to aperiodic seizures.

The *learning theorists* maintain that disturbance is a learned condition and, as such, can be unlearned and appropriate behavior relearned. Emphasis here is placed upon changing those events in the environment that are contributing to and/or maintaining a child's maladaptive behavior.

A *sociological* definition would not recognize individual disturbance. The society itself is "sick" for contributing to the conflict experienced by the individual. In this perspective the individual is a victim of the larger malady perpetuated by society.

An *ecological* definition of conflict recognizes the interactive effect of man on his environment and, in turn, the environment on the man. Conflict is recognized as being internal, but significantly maintained by the environment.

A *counter-theorist* would say that all of the traditionally entrenched institutions have contributed to individual conflict. Counter-theorists advocate humanistic approaches to enhance the individual's feeling of self-worth. Individuals become conflicted when denied opportunities to become self-actualized.

Why then is there not a single, universally accepted definition of *conflict*? Most assuredly there have been attempts to generate one. Bower's (1969) definition is being quoted more and more. The fact that his definition has been incorporated into PL 94-142 is going to add to its increased use as "the" definition of conflict used in educational settings. This does not say anything about its acceptance or use in the medical field, social work field, or in mental health. Bower's definition refers to children that exhibit one or more of the following five characteristics to a marked degree and over an extended time:

1. An inability to learn, which cannot be explained by intellectual, sensory, or health factors.
2. An inability to build or maintain satisfactory interpersonal relationships with peers and teachers.
3. Inappropriate types of behavior or feelings under normal conditions.
4. A general pervasive mood of unhappiness or depression.
5. A tendency to develop physical symptoms, pains, or fears associated with personal or school problems (pp. 22-23).

Kauffman (1977) points to the following reasons when discussing problems associated with deriving a "single" definition of conflict:

1. *Measurement.* With so much individual variability, how does one devise a

test to quantify human behavior objectively?

2. *Orientation.* Already discussed previously, but various theoretical perspectives cause individuals to subscribe to different etiologies of conflict.
3. *Range.* Children can exhibit *excesses* or *deficiencies* in behavior, and this is difficult to incorporate into a definition
4. *Variability.* Factors such as a behavior that is acceptable in certain settings and not in others, or the fact that a child's behavior is viewed as adaptive until he goes to school, add to the problem. Additional considerations include how much of the child's waking hours are engaged in maladaptive behaviors, and are the problems acute (after a death or divorce) or chronic (long-term) in their development and manifestation?
5. *Effects of Labeling.* This is an issue widely discussed today, but also of vital consideration in deriving a definition of conflict. If a behavior is labeled and defined, what will be the long-term effect of that label on the child? Will it be a cross to be born forever?

What is to be done then? Four suggestions are made:

1. There needs to be a recommendation by the National Advisory Committee on Handicapped Children for a definition of *conflict* much like their 1968 Report on Learning Disabilities. This definition ought to represent a compromise definition that all fields involved can contribute to and can live with.
2. It should be kept in mind that there are exceptions to everything, and as such there will always be a child somewhere that does not fit any and/or every definition. This does not mean that everything else that has been achieved was wrong, but rather should allow us to accept the uniqueness and individuality of man.
3. Avoid labels at all costs. No one deserves the effects of labeling.
4. Accept conflict as normal and acceptable. This perspective recognizes conflict as an inability to cope temporarily, and allows the individual the freedom and the right to experience his conflict unbegrudged, and to allow others to help him learn coping skills when necessary.

The next issue is not as simplistic as is possibly depicted here, but in fact consists of two inextricably related facets. However, for purposes of examination, an attempt will be made to discuss them separately. The overall issue is the lack of a single universally accepted and used unified intervention model for use with EC children. The dual nature of the issue hinges on (1) whether to stress academics or behavior as the intervention approach with EC children, and (2) the perennial argument involving whether to take a psychodynamic or learning theory emphasis in intervention.

The debate over whether to stress academics or behavior has been occurring primarily since intervention with EC children went public — public schools that is! Prior to that time the problem was not acute for two reasons. Before the advent of EC classes in public schools, if a child was experiencing emotional problems, he sought help from mental health professionals outside the school, whose task it was to ameliorate the child's emotional problems. Academics did not even enter into consideration. Too, in the rare cases where there were EC classes in the public schools, a psychologist was typically hired to intercede in "crisis" situations, again with no emphasis towards academics.

Examining the academics end more closely, the prevailing notion has been that if one could simply get the child operating on his grade level, then somehow all of his problems would vanish. The underlying assumption was that the deviant behavior was really school related, tied to a faulty match between the child's abilities and the teacher's expectations of him. All one had to do under this hypothesis was assess the child's strengths and weaknesses, individualize a plan of intervention, most of which would be skill development (academic, not behavior), and make it highly structured, sequential, with small steps, of high interest, amply reinforced with appropriate rewards, and of short duration. After all of this the child would be miraculously cured of his emotional problems without ever once having worked on them in the context in which they existed or presented themselves! Is this not somewhat naive?

The scenario to this has been the increasing acknowledgment that this approach, although generally successful in the acquisition of new skills, has not performed ideally in changing students' behaviors in nonstructured, nonreinforced environments. Yet, if this approach has not worked, why have teachers not changed to something that does work or at least shows more promise of working? Why is it still an issue? One reason is student containment, maturation, and promotion. By keeping the student contained, or rather, so occupied as not to allow an opportunity to misbehave, then outwardly he must not have any problems. Too, as children mature, many either outgrow or learn to compensate for their emotional shortcomings. And finally, they advance to the next grade, where they become someone else's problem. The result of all this is twofold. The child progresses yearly from grade to grade and is left on his own to correct his problem(s), which usually does not occur; hence, the problem gets worse and worse. The second effect is that for the reasons cited previously, the approach *appears* to work. Yet we really do not know, do we?

However there exists another significant consideration explaining why the academic argument persists. Academics is what administrators charged with evaluating programs know best and, therefore, is what they insist upon. There continues to be inordinate amounts of pressure placed on administrators to be accountable for their various programs. The easiest way to measure progress is to compare changes in grade level scores, and these scores are not affected if a child has spent an entire year in play therapy or in rap sessions attempting to get a handle on his emotional struggles. Administrators have not been shown ways to assess objective gains in behavior, and the reason for this has been that none have ever existed! So, the insistence of many special education coordinators setting up classes for EC children for the first time has been to follow the academic model of the LD teacher, whose goals are primarily academic and not necessarily behavior oriented.

Additionally, if behavior is emphasized, not necessarily over academics, but surely concurrently, then there must be a uniform means of presentation and accountability, i.e. a behavior curriculum. A behavior curriculum ought to consist of at least the same major elements found in an academic curriculum. These elements would be assessment, goals, objectives, activities, and evaluation.

What kinds of behavior curriculums exist? Of the ones that do, the following three are mentioned because of their wide use and significant contributions to the field. They are Hewett and Taylor's (1980) *Levels of Learning Competence*, Wood's (1975) *Developmental Therapy*, and Stephens's (1978) *Social Skills Curriculum.*

Hewett and Taylor's (1980) *Levels of Learning Competence* is incorporated into an overall intervention strategy commonly referred to as "the engineered classroom." The engineered classroom was the founding concept behind the Santa Monica Project of the mid-1960s. Hewett and Taylor believed that the various theoretical models discussed previously were particularly inadequate in showing how to develop a model for intervention in an educational setting. Further, they believed that the strategies necessary to fuse academic and behavior goals into an educational setting were developmental in sequence. The result was the developmental levels of learning competence shown in Figure 1-1.

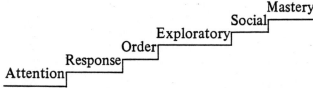

Figure 1-1. Hewett and Taylor's *Levels of Learning Competence.* Copyright 1968 by Allyn and Bacon, Inc. All rights reserved. Reprinted by permission Allyn and Bacon, Inc.

They have taken this hierarchy and developed assessment procedures, objectives, activities, and evaluation. They have also developed the necessary support documentation for teacher use and spell out very amply the how-to-implement procedures. And their book is full of educational activities too. Mary Wood's (1975) *Developmental Therapy,* like Hewett and Taylor's, is also developmental in nature. It derives from the Rutland model developed at the University of Georgia. The developmental therapy model has extensive support systems and spends a great deal of time supporting the child as he moves back into the regular classroom. Wood's developmental goals are divided into four areas: behavior, communication, socialization, and academics. Each area is further divided into stages 1 – 5, with Stage 1 being the lowest stage requiring the most support and smallest ratio of students to teachers. The four areas times the five stages form a 4 by 5 matrix with one goal in each box and with each goal having additional objectives. The model has been received favorably enough that the entire state of Georgia has adopted statewide psychoeducational centers modeled after the Rutland model with its developmental therapy approach.

Stephens's (1978) *Social Skills* curriculum is a subunit of the very comprehensive Directive Teaching Instructional Management System (DTIMS). It was written in response to helping teachers fill out IEP's. The curriculum covers the areas of reading, handwriting, spelling, arithmetic, and social skills. Each area has respectively 267, 65, 19, 317, and 140 objectives. Stephens provides assessment data and teaching strategies. The social skills component advocates three kinds of teaching strategies: social modeling, social reinforcement, and contingency contracting to achieve the various goals. The goals are shown next.

Stephens's Social Skills Goals*

Environmental

> Care of Environment — 5 objectives
> Dealing with Emergency — 3 objectives
> Lunchroom — 3 objectives
> Movement Around Environment — 4 objectives

Interpersonal Relations

> Accepting Authority — 5 objectives
> Coping with Conflict — 6 objectives
> Gaining Attention — 6 objectives
> Greeting Others — 7 objectives
> Helping Others — 7 objectives
> Making Conversation — 8 objectives
> Organized Play — 4 objectives
> Positive Attitude Toward Others — 3 objectives
> Play Informally — 5 objectives
> Care of Property — 4 objectives

Self-Related

> Accepting Consequences — 3 objectives
> Ethical Behavior — 4 objectives
> Expressing Feelings — 2 objectives
> Positive Attitude Towards Self — 4 objectives
> Responsible Behavior — 7 objectives
> Self-Care — 3 objectives

Task-Related

> Asking and Answering Questions — 4 objectives
> Attending Behaviors — 6 objectives
> Classroom Discussion — 6 objectives
> Completing Tasks — 4 objectives
> Following Directions — 4 objectives
> Group Activities — 5 objectives
> Independent Work — 3 objectives
> On-Task Behavior — 6 objectives
> Performing Before Others — 5 objectives
> Quality of Work — 4 objectives

No single curriculum can be all things to all teachers, just as one theory of intervention could never really answer all questions about EC children. However, the above curriculums are excellent, as is further evidenced by their widespread use. And yet even these three differ from each other, and occasionally, a child in conflict still drops through the cracks as not fitting or benefiting from the curriculum. Hence, we have taken frequently recurring behaviors identified by teachers and have organized them into the *Conflict Resolution Curriculum* (CRC) (*see* Chap. 2).

The CRC was the outgrowth of examining various avenues to develop an application model based on the model of conflict espoused by Linkous (1974). Linkous's model is referred to as a *Transactional Systems Approach* (TSA). The TSA (discussed in more detail later in this chapter) is one attempt to put manageability into the unification issue, because if there is no agreement as to what constitutes conflict, or how to deal effectively with it, then how is one to proceed in developing a behavior-oriented curriculum? The answer is to start with a unified model or approach and then build upon it. Towards this goal there are at least three schools of thought: the purists, the acknowledgers, and the effectors (author's terminology). The issue is the sometimes strongly delineated problem of whether to take a psychodynamic approach to behavior or a learning theory approach. To a purist it is one or the other, with absolutely no tolerance for views espoused by the other side. Two frequent comments sum up each side's arguments. To a learning theorist, behavior modification is life: it explains how behaviors can be unlearned and adaptive behaviors relearned and, at the same time, clearly shows how and why humans are willing to do good work for the recognition attained, or why one will endure a frumpy old professor for an entire semester just to get a good grade, or why we do jobs we do not necessarily want to do just to get a check at the end of the month, etc. To a psychodynamic proponent, learning theory has yet to show its ability to consistently internalize behaviors or how to generalize from one situation to another. Further, it is argued, learning theorists will justify any means to achieve the end and will totally disavow the client's feelings, the development of insight into the nature of his problems, and further, make no mention of the "quality" of life derived from appreciating one's accomplishments in achieving adaptive behavior.

An acknowledger meanwhile subscribes to one view or the other, but is cognizant enough to acknowledge that his/her own theoretical perspective does not supply all the answers or approaches necessary to ameliorate conflict. However, other than admitting that there might exist some credence in the other view, an acknowledger typically does not venture forth to discover those merits because then he might have to re-examine his positions, which he is not particularly inclined to do.

The last group, the effectors, admits that both camps have strong points and that both go a long way towards explaining behavior, but at the same time each alone is unable to supply all the answers. Hence, the effector's approach is to use both approaches to effect positive growth in children in conflict. This group's in-use theory (Argyris and Schön, 1977) most closely approximates a unified intervention model. Their actions denote a consolidation of models, without actually espousing this theory as a unification model.

This argument between learning theorists and psychodynamicists is probably the central issue preventing generalized acceptance of a unified approach in working with EC children and, therefore, a unified curriculum. Without being aware of it, most good effectors probably routinely practice a synthesis approach in helping problem children. This is also called an *eclectic approach,* of which there are two kinds. The first is called the *"green-thumb"* approach. In this approach the teacher and/or therapist uses whatever works; there is no consideration of why or of what possible rippling effects might occur. Also, there is no consideration of what technique works better on one child than on another, which leads to a technique having, for instance, a 50 percent effectiveness rate and no thought as to why. In this approach there is no prior selectivity about which technique to use; one simply has an arsenal of weapons to bombard the child with and hopes that one works.

The inappropriateness of this approach ought to be apparent. If one is working with a highly volatile child or a withdrawn child, one would want to be very discriminant in selecting how to work with that child rather than randomly using something that worked all right for another different child. Also, this approach really does not allow the teacher or therapist the freedom of choice that at first glance might appear to be there but is not, because the teacher-therapist really lacks selectivity in choosing techniques.

The second kind of eclecticism is more theoretically oriented, not theoretical in application necessarily, but at least more in underlying bases. In working with disturbed children the teacher wants the freedom of choice to use anything that is going to work, be it learning theory or psychodynamic in nature. At the same time, the teacher ought to have a reason for selecting his/her course of intervention other than saying, "Well, it has worked before." While agreement on one unified theory may never be reached, it is possible to talk about an eclectic approach to intervention that is carefully thought out and judiciously used. One such model that has been proffered as eclectic has been the Rhodes (1972) ecological model. The ecological model examines the interaction between man and his environment. The model acknowledges the effect each has on the other and defines conflict as problems with the interface between the two. Obviously the internal nature of man affects his reactions with the environment, and likewise, the environment acts upon the man. The intervention is ecological in nature, i.e. change is effected in the individual with further change and support established in his ecosystem.

Another eclectic model is the TSA (Linkous, 1974). The TSA addresses the multi-influences on a child's emotional conflicts. The basic premise is that man is an action being. During the course of man's actions, he encounters forces and actions acting upon him, hence the term *transactional*. Since man does not operate in a vacuum, nature has shown us that life is orderly and systematic. There are rules that govern behavior, and theoretically there ought to exist a finite system of behaviors. If this system exists, then by studying it man ought to be able to predict behavior, and subsequently, that which can be predicted can be planned for. Systems theory has repeatedly demonstrated that any universe of behaviors or actions is composed of various subsystems. These subsystems interact and mesh with the other systems. If one subsystem is affected, the status of all the remaining subsystems is influenced. Putting this systems approach in the realm of behavior and examining the green-thumb approach discussed earlier, one should see the underlying fallacy of the green-thumb approach. If a behavior is selected to be acted upon (e.g. changing a child's out-of-seat behavior), and behavior modification is always employed, then two things have occurred. One, the teacher or therapist has forfeited his freedom of choice by always adopting a learning theory approach to change overt behavior. Two, there is no thought about what effect the therapist's actions will have on the other subsystems, resulting in diminished efficacy and invited criticism about why learning theory does not work when in fact it is a very powerful agent.

However, in the TSA, one has increased selectivity. This is true because the therapist can pull from the entire array of techniques available to work with EC children and, additionally, knows why he has selected the technique he has. The TSA is composed of three subsystems or subsets: *mental, manifest,* and *material.* The mental subset encompasses those ideas typically covered under a psychodynamic model. The *mental* domain is concerned with the feeling or internal being. The *manifest* subset deals with manifest overt behavior and how the environment influences and/or maintains these behaviors. The concern is not primarily with internal feelings or motivations but with changing overt actions. This is recognizable as learning theory in origin. The final subset is the *material* and is concerned with the biophysiological nature of man and his behavior. Hence, with the recognition that each subset is separate but tied to the other two, the range of places to start with EC children is three times greater than with the traditional adherence to one of the models of conflict. The transactional nature of this system's approach can be seen in the following example.

A child comes to school cranky, loud, and volatile. The learning theorist approaches the problem by using contingency contracting. If the child quietly enters the room and gets on task, his reward will be ten minutes of the teacher's undivided attention at recess. The psychotherapist approaches the problem by having weekly rap sessions with the child to help the child develop insight into the whys of his actions. The TSA therapist, after assessment of the situation, not unlike the other two would have done, says, "let's give this child a warm breakfast." This affects the material subsystem. The child eats and feels better. He's now able to attend in class. The teacher notices this and responds positively towards the child. The child's self-esteem is stroked, and he responds by improved in-seat behavior and diminished acting-out behaviors. We now have an upward bound spiral of positive feeding positive, and all three subsystems have become involved. The *material* was acted upon, and the *mental* was affected, which in turn influenced the child's *manifest* behavior. The question becomes, why would anyone purposely limit themselves to just one course of action via one intervention theory or model, i.e. psychodynamic, learning, sociologic, or biophysiologic?

The TSA advocates the term "emotional conflict" as an alternative to the more traditional "emotional disturbance and behavior disorders." As mentioned earlier the state of Alabama has adopted the EC terminology to refer to ED or BD kids. EC children are said to be emotionally conflicted. In using the EC term, the TSA recognizes three kinds of conflict. There is internal conflict as when one is trying to decide between right and wrong or making a life-affecting decision. There is also the kind of conflict between two people as when spouses disagree, and finally, there is conflict between man and his environment as is generated by overcrowded living conditions, the bureaucratic system, or a too-small paycheck at the end of the month. The real impetus underlying this view of conflict is its inescapability. Everybody experiences conflicts — some to a lesser degree than others — but we are all in this together. Conflict is a concept that allows the individual to be empathic towards the less fortunate or more conflicted soul. It is no longer something that happens to the other fellow. This view helps the interventioner maintain perspective because it allows for subjective identification and objectivity, too. It is objective in that the therapist still retains the selectivity of intervention strategies, but employs them having a better appreciation for what the conflicted child is experiencing.

Implicit, too, in the concept of EC is *growth*. There is some argument that without conflict there is no growth, and one indication of growth or emotional adaptiveness is how individuals resolve their conflicts. If life presents no conflicts, people become complacent. With complacency comes mediocrity and no growth. It is like the analogy that without highs there can be no lows, or you cannot appreciate winning until you have also lost.

Emotional Conflict is defined as *the absence of adaptive behavior*. Adaptive behavior is defined in the following equation (Linkous, 1974):

LINKOUS' DEFINITION OF EMOTIONAL CONFLICT

$$AB = CS + PV \geq ED + SV$$
$$MB \text{ or } EC = CS + PV < ED + SV$$
$$\text{where } AB = \text{Adaptive Behavior}$$

MB = Maladaptive Behavior
CS = Coping Skills
PV = Personal Values
ED = Environmental Demands
SV = Societal Values

IMPLICATIONS FOR THE FUTURE OF THE FIELD

Where does the foregoing discussion lead? Has anything been resolved? Events and issues have been raised; the individual resolution of which is not always apparent. Has anything truly significant been contributed to the field in the recent past? For an area so large as EC, new ideas have been minimal at best! Yet, if one reviews one's field of endeavor and is critical, is there not a concomitant responsibility to offer new direction or at least another option?

Is not one of the major goals of intervention with children in conflict to show them new options? And if the field of EC itself is in conflict, then it too should look for new options. The option offered here is to build upon the theoretical organization of conflict offered by Linkous (1974). This organization is called a *systems approach* because of the transactional nature of man. The emphasis of this book is to apply the TSA to a behavior curriculum. The result is the Conflict Resolution Curriculum (CRC).

However, the CRC is not a panacea. Additionally, simply because a curriculum is in hand, i.e. the CRC, there is no guarantee it will work. Necessary to any successful effort is an underlying philosophy of action. The philosophy of intervention for the CRC is presented in Chapter 3, which follows the presentation of the CRC in Chapter 2. Chapter 4 gives case studies of the CRC in operation.

THE CONFLICT RESOLUTION CURRICULUM

INTRODUCTION

THE basic aim in developing the Conflict Resolution Curriculum (CRC) was to aid the already beleaguered classroom teacher in working with EC children. What was sought was a systematic procedure to plan intervention and to have that plan reflected in the child's IEP. The premises upon which the CRC was founded were threefold.

1. *It must be simple.* Simplicity underscores the usability of anything. It must be simple, too, for use with IEP's, as teachers are looking for procedures that expedite the writing and implementation of their IEP's.
2. *It must be comprehensive.* In order to maximize practicality, a curriculum must reflect the widest range of presenting behaviors. As much as is possible the curriculum must attempt to plan for any conceivable behavior problem that the teacher might encounter.
3. *It must be general.* A good curriculum ought to be designed to aid teachers to adapt that curriculum to their style of teaching, to their students, and to the environment in which intervention is planned. By being general the teacher can add to or delete from the curriculum without affecting the design of the curriculum or its functionality.

In striving to meet these aims several recurring problems persisted. The question was how to develop a single curriculum that would account for the multitude of facets that must be dealt with in successful intervention with problem children. The most recurring problems were:

1. *Age of child.* How do you plan a curriculum that allows for age differences? Age affects how teachers develop their intervention strategy. Procedures vary if the child is younger or older.
2. *Degree of involvement.* The degree of conflict determines strategy. If a child is severely conflicted, behavior modification is probably the more appropriate strategy to follow, whereas if the child is mildly or moderately involved, then psychodynamic techniques might be suggested.
3. *Approach of intervention.* The teacher or therapist's own biases must be taken into consideration. If a curriculum pushes one approach to the sole exclusion of others, then it is destined to fail from the beginning. The curriculum should allow interventioners to use whatever style they feel most comfortable with.
4. *Locus of control.* With young children or severely conflicted children the locus of control should be external. By external, the teacher or therapist

structures the environment to limit choices or decisions by the child. It is strongly debatable whether a six-year-old should bear the full responsibility for his every action, the same being true with the severely involved child. Too, older children should be learning to assume that responsibility, and, hence, be developing an internal locus of control. With external control, learning theory is used to structure the environment and limit options, while psychodynamic theory is more appropriate in developing internal control.

5. *Setting of intervention.* Where is the curriculum to be implemented? With severe EC, it is most probably in a self-contained setting. With mild to moderate EC, it is most probably in a combination of EC resource room and the mainstream. A curriculum should be workable in both settings.

6. *Support system.* Does the curriculum include the means to support the EC child in his natural environment? What kinds of supports exist to maintain or reinforce new behaviors that have been or are being acquired? Is the child allowed to practice his new behaviors where he ultimately is expected to exhibit them?

Thus, these considerations were included in the CRC. Where they are not obvious to the user of the curriculum, they are implied. This becomes part of the rationale for using the CRC. The teacher should constantly ask himself whether all of these have been kept in mind while implementing the curriculum.

Intense examination of the above facets resulted in the following three goals. These overall curriculum goals were felt to reflect most accurately the directions in which EC teachers would want to move their students. The EC teacher wants to accomplish any or all of these three goals. The goals are:

1. *Improve manifest behavior.* Problems of which are characterized by overt actions (too much or too little of) or physical expression. These behaviors are typically detrimental, directed towards self, others, or the environment. These behaviors involve physical action, irrespective of why, and are action oriented.

2. *Improve intrapersonal communication skills.* Problems of which are characterized by negative personal feelings, lack of self-worth, and actions directed towards self. This would include having inappropriate thought patterns, yet does not require the presence of another person to occur, and is feeling oriented.

3. *Improve interpersonal communication skills.* Problems of which are characterized by verbal or nonverbal communication with others or the environment. Additionally includes the expression of thoughts and requires the presence of another person to occur.

The individual objectives were derived from the problem areas under each goal (*see* Summary of Goals). The problem areas represent clusters of behaviors used to delineate the various gradations of behaviors that would typically be thought to fall under that particular goal. Critical to the development of the CRC was an attempt to mesh assessment and intervention. One of the major shortcomings in special education has been the transition between the assessment of a child's abilities (and in this case his behaviors) and the eventual intervention with that child. For this reason the problem areas and their descriptors were listed immediately following the goal statement. This was done to facilitate the transition from behavior ratings compiled during the assessment and placement of the EC child to an intervention plan. The teacher is able to find the problem area that most accurately reflects the problem(s) that the child is having. Then all that is required is to select the appropriate objective(s) found following each problem area. Some overlap will be evident; this occurs because of the inability to separate behaviors clearly. There will always be overlap of behaviors in dealing with EC children. This is acceptable and does not affect the integrity of the CRC.

The activities that follow from the objectives are not meant to be all inclusive. They are meant to be illustrative of the possibilities for meeting the objectives. The generation of activities is where teachers are most creative. Teachers are encouraged to take the CRC objectives and, by using the activities as a guide, develop their own activities to match their unique situations. Too, by developing their own activities and hence adding to the CRC, teachers have more of an investment in seeing that the curriculum is successful in its implementation.

IMPLEMENTATION

The CRC was *not* designed for the teacher to select one to three activities and then do just those activities during a 40-50-minute class period. Even though the EC child is in the special class for help with his behavior problems, academics must also be dealt with. Also, successful teachers know that a variety of activities are more likely to insure success and maintain attention than are one or two activities. Academics frequently afford the teacher the medium through which to address the child's problems. But, too, behavior remediation should always be the uppermost goal of the EC teacher.

To obtain maximum efficacy from the CRC, a "many-mini" approach is strongly advocated. A many-mini approach is one in which the teacher designs many activities into the daily schedule and then offers them to the child in a minimum-time frame. This approach is believed to be the best because it affords the best opportunity to change behavior. No one likes preaching, yet this is what many students perceive to be happening when they are told, or asked to talk about, or asked why they are manifesting a particular behavior. Teachers should recall that a child in conflict is like an adult with bad habits. We are aware we have the habits, do not like to be reminded that we have these habits, and are more inclined to change those habits, not by being preached at, but rather by constant, gentle reminders that allow us gradually to get new habits engrained in the place of the old ones. This is where behavior modification programs generally fail. They are great at showing us our bad habits and are great at getting us to practice those new habits. Behavior modification fails at helping us to internalize those new habits over the long haul when there is no one there to reinforce us. So by initially discussing the behaviors that the teacher and student want to change and then by incorporating many mini-lessons into the daily activities, the teacher has done everything that can be done to maximize effective intervention. Then it becomes a matter of time to see if the child can internalize by getting the support he needs in his natural environment to maintain those new behaviors.

THE CONFLICT RESOLUTION CURRICULUM

Summary of Goals

GOAL 1. *Improved Manifest Behavior*

PROBLEM AREA 1A. Student engages in activities that prevent him/her from interacting in a faciI atory manner with the environment, yet are non-disruptive to normal classroom activities.

PROBLEM AREA 1B. Student engages in actions not directed toward others but intended to disrupt, or actually results in classroom disruptions.

PROBLEM AREA 1C. Student engages in actions physically directed towards others/environment.

PROBLEM AREA 1D. Student engages in inappropriate activities that are biologically rooted and manifested.

GOAL 2. *Improved Intrapersonal Communication Skills*

PROBLEM AREA 2A. Inappropriate perceptions of one's feelings.

PROBLEM AREA 2B. Inappropriate perceptions of one's body.

PROBLEM AREA 2C. Inappropriate perceptions of one's coping skills.

PROBLEM AREA 2D. Inappropriate perceptions of one's social responsibilities.

PROBLEM AREA 2E. Inappropriate perceptions of others and the environment.

GOAL 3. *Improved Interpersonal Communication Skills*

PROBLEM AREA 3A. Student is not receiving communication from the environment.

PROBLEM AREA 3B. Student is not comprehending communication attempts.

PROBLEM AREA 3C. Student does not respond appropriately to outside communication.

GOAL 1: IMPROVED MANIFEST BEHAVIOR

Definition: Characterized by overt actions (too much or too little of) or physical expression, typically detrimental, directed towards self, others, or the environment. Involves physical action, irrespective of why.

Problem Area 1A: Child engages in activities that prevent him/her from interacting in a facilitatory manner with the environment, yet is non-disruptive to normal activities.

Common Descriptors of this Problem Area:

- lazy
- underachieving
- poor attendance
- poor concentration
- short attention span
- restless
- overactive

- poor task completion
- distractable
- problems following directions
- fiddles with objects
- daydreams
- inappropriate use of time

Objectives	Activities	Evaluation
1. Student will demonstrate knowledge of sequences of events required to successfully complete assigned task.	1. a. When given instructions student will correctly recite them back to teacher. b. Teacher verbally walks through instructions with student. c. Have student do task analysis of routine activities. d. Give student jumbled instructions or sequenced activities on tape or written out and have him put into proper order.	1. a. Student is able to recite, list or demonstrate correct sequences of test situations with ____ % of accuracy in ____ (secs, mins) over a period of time or given situation. b. Student will examine sequence of activities and will match or identify the activity to which related. c. Student will correctly (____ % accuracy) task analyze given task.
2. Student will select appropriate materials to complete assigned task.	2. a. Ask student what materials they would need to do a long list of routine tasks. b. Give student lists of materials to gather for the teacher. c. Given three complete lists of materials, student correctly selects which one is correct for any given assignment. Have student include reasons for his rejection of alternatives as well as why he chose the one he did. d. Have student distribute materials for assignments once he correctly identifies what is needed.	2. a. Given task, student successfully (____ % of time) obtains appropriate materials. b. Student will be able to correctly (____ % of time) distribute to class material for each of their activities. c. Student verbalizes proper care of selected materials.

Note: There is not necessarily an item-by-item match-up across objectives-activities evaluation, i.e. evaluation 10 is not just for activity 10.

3. Student will be able to care for and organize materials for personal use.

e. Have discussions that show students use of different materials and routes to achieve similar goals.

f. Show student how to locate materials, e.g. the use of librarians, community resources, other teachers.

g. Stress the need for flexibility in accepting availability of materials.

3. a. Discuss benefits of organization.

b. Have student find examples of organized and unorganized activities and people, then discuss which ones he sees to be more chaotic.

c. Have student compare himself to other people that he thinks are organized. Have the student notice the similarities and differences between him and those people and develop a plan to improve his own personal organization.

d. Give assignments with part of the instructions missing. Can student figure them out? Make activities highly motivating to child. If he cannot complete the task discuss his frustration and how to resolve his frustration.

e. Have student discuss his feelings when he has wanted to do something fun and could not because someone let him down or something was broken. Then have him discuss how others must feel when he breaks or takes something that the other person needed to complete the task.

f. How does student feel when his favorite possession is lost, broken, or stolen?

a. Student keeps log, initialed by teacher, of whether or not he arrives prepared and ready to do work.

4. Student will be able to begin, carry-out, and terminate assigned tasks in an orderly manner.

4. a. Design fun games or activities. Then announce the beginning, ending, and transition time allotments. Then conduct activity holding child to time lines.

b. Discuss use of time and organization of time in the personal life of the student.

4. a. Given task or assignment, student begins appropriately within _____ (secs, mins) _____ % of the time.

c. Study and discuss effects of specific examples that run on schedules and what would happen if they did not run on time, e.g., TV shows, classes, radio, buses, airlines, amusement parks, records, etc.

d. Study how to organize personal time.

e. Study how to estimate time necessary for different tasks.

f. Do time and motion studies of activities. This could include studies by the student of routine classroom tasks. Then set these time limits as goals for comparisons. Then have student keep logs of his actual time used for activities and then discuss why the time goals were not met by student, and what needs to be done to meet the goals.

5. Student will be able to change from one assigned task to the next smoothly and without incident.

6. Student will utilize his time appropriately, be it work or leisure time.

7. Student will be able to increasingly delay gratification for successful task completion.

8. Student will maintain himself on the assigned task regardless of outside distractions.

9. Student will gradually increase his attending or concentration time on assigned tasks.

5-9.

a. Have student engage in endurance activities.

b. Determine how quickly the student can complete a task.

c. Determine how long the student can maintain monotonous task.

d. Do games/activities with outside distractions. Compare the student's ability to do task with and without distractions. While he is engaged in the activity, have him discuss effects of distractions on him at that time.

e. Have students do simultaneous activities. Usually competition enters into the activity and once behind the child quits. Instead, have the child talk about what he feels, why, and alternatives.

5-9.

a. Given task, student maintains a concentration time of _____ (sec, mins) on doing the task and is able to do this _____ % of time.

b. When commanded to terminate a task the student terminates within _____ secs, _____ % of time correctly or appropriately.

c. Student is able to complete transition in _____ (secs/mins) with fewer than _____ (1-2, etc.) distractions.

d. Student keeps log of time required to complete tasks; reviews with teacher why variances exist.

e. Teacher assigns time frames for task completions, and compares these estimates against student's record of actual time spent.

f. Student keeps a log of how his time is utilized and budgeted. Teacher and student review log together to determine appropriate utilization of time.

g. Student and teacher tabulate separately and then compare length of time between completion of task and receipt of reward. Student keeps log of when he completed task and when and how he was rewarded.

Problem Area 1B: Student engages in actions not physically directed toward others, but intended to disrupt or actually results in disruptions.

Common Descriptors of this Problem Area:

- repetitious behavior
- ritualistic behavior
- perfectionistic
- obsessive-compulsive
- steals
- inappropriate attention-seeking behaviors
- no group participation
- nonconformity
- temper tantrums
- excessive excitability
- tardiness

Objectives	Activities	Evaluation
1. Student is able to list his disruptive habits and/or his inappropriate attention-seeking behaviors.	1. a. Student describes appropriate behavior expected of people in different settings. b. Classmates role play different roles and their corresponding role-expectation behaviors. c. Teacher previously establishes with the class, and then practices for the time, when she says — "OK, everybody freeze! Now, Johnny, describe what is going on right now and how you are appropriately or inappropriately reacting. Who's in control of your behavior right now? Where's the power right now?" d. Student is assigned to find examples in other people of his target behavior. This behavior should already be worked out with the teacher. Once the student and teacher find examples of the targeted behavior in others, they should discuss why the model student is able to carry out the behavior, and how to apply those skills to the student having problems.	1. a. Student correctly verbalizes his inappropriate action within ⎯⎯ secs after being confronted by teacher for engaging in such activity. b. When confronted with his inappropriate behavior student initiates predetermined alternative within ⎯⎯ secs/mins.
2. Student will verbalize and implement alternatives to his usual inappropriate attention-seeking behaviors.	2. a. The following sequence should be incorporated as a unit: • Teacher and student identify student's inappropriate behavior (no more than 2 at a time). • Teacher and student select adaptive target behaviors to ameliorate maladaptive behaviors.	2. a. Student is able to verbalize or record instances in which, unprompted, he engaged in prearranged alternatives.

3. Student participates appropriately with others in a group setting.	• Teacher and student identify antecedent and response patterns of the student that result in his inappropriate behavior. Student then logs frequency of target behavior upon teacher prompt. • Teacher and student verbalize alternatives to student's usual response patterns. • When confronted by teacher concerning his inappropriate behavior, student selects which alternative he chooses to carry out, and logs results. • Student implements alternatives in regular class with support of regular teacher via a monitoring system with the resource teacher. 3. a. Teacher and students study the basics of group dynamics. Young children can practice social roles and expectations for them. b. Older student could study groups in depth: their composition, who leads, who follows, how to influence, how to get group and individual needs met, how to react to inappropriate participation. This can be accomplished through different role-play activities, and studies of other groups that the students are not in.	3. a. Upon completion of group activity, a majority of the group report positive participation from student. b. Student verbalizes the extent and quality of appropriate participation in group.

Problem Area 1C: Student engages in actions physically directed towards others/environment.

Common Descriptors of
this Problem Area:

- acting-out
- disrupts others
- no self-control
- aggressiveness
- no respect for property
- no respect for rights of others
- teases
- sexual aggression
- bullying
- destructive

Objectives	Activities	Evaluation
1. Student verbalizes and exhibits acceptable alternatives to his usual physical aggressions. This is to include (1) stopping himself, or (2) removing himself from the situation, or (3) finding acceptable avenues for physically venting his anger.	1. a. Student and teacher establish student's usual behavior patterns which result in physical aggressions. b. Student and teacher then explore a list of possible alternatives for the student to his physical aggressions. c. Student and teacher practice possible alternatives. d. Teacher verbally directs student to alternative when he's upset. e. Student moves to alternative upon verbal cue from teacher. f. Student verbalizes benefits of newly implemented alternatives when he has cooled down.	1. Student and teacher select observable alternatives to student's usual physical aggressions, then tabulate number of times student does not exercise alternative. When the percent of times he does exceeds the percent of times he does not without cue from teacher, then child will have met his goal.
2. Student demonstrates respect for physical and psychological space of others.	2. a. Does student know what physical and psychological spaces are? b. How does one violate someone else's space? c. How do physical and psychological space relate to one's sense of security? d. What is security? Is it different for different people? e. Do physical and psychological space vary in size for different people? Do exercise to demonstrate this. Stand one student in one space and have him engage in conversation with another student. Have the second student gradually approach the first student until they are almost touching. Students observing take notes on each talker's reactions as they moved closer. Then class discusses reactions and feelings with the two students for comparisons and applications to other situations.	2. a. Teacher establishes rate of violation of physical or psychological space by student towards others during base rate period. b. After implementation of program, goal will be attained when violation drops below _____ % of base rate.

3. Student will not encourage misbehavior in others by his actions or words.

3. a. Take a real-life classroom disruption and analyze how the chain reaction occurred, how the student's actions influenced others, and the ultimate placement of responsibility for individual behavior.

   b. Help other students see how they are being manipulated by the student in question.

   c. Heavily reinforce the idea of mutual responsibility for behavior.

   d. This is a good time to introduce the concept of the use of individual power and in not allowing others to get you upset.

3. Evaluation criteria should be established based on the degree of the problem and the reality of expectation of change in behavior.

4. Student is able to deal successfully with competition.

4. a. Above all teach, train, or develop a unique skill in a child that gives him something to be best in. This one skill alone will go a long way towards building his self-concept and helping him deal successfully with competition. An excellent source for information on competition is to be found in Hewett's *The Emotionally Disturbed Child in the Classroom* (1968 Edition).

   b. Have the class make a study of the pervasiveness of competition in society.

   c. The teacher might bring in various people who deal with competition daily, e.g. athletes, musicians, newspaperpersons, models, etc., to discuss how they deal with competition.

   d. Students discuss how competition effects them in their daily lives and how they deal with competition.

   e. Teacher helps student determine if acceptable alternatives to traditional competition exist and then helps the student implement and practice those alternatives.

   f. Student keeps log to note when he was in a competitive situation that was causing him some problems, and how he resolved the problem.

4. Evaluation criteria should be established based on the degree of the problem and the reality of expectation of change in behavior.

Objective	Activities	Evaluation
5. Student will engage in appropriate sex role behaviors.	5. a. Do a unit on sex education, but let parents and administration give approval first, if required. b. Discuss sex roles — what are they, how do we get them, how have they changed over the years? How do they change with age? What are society's expectations as to male and female roles? Have students role play different roles, ages, and stages.	5. Student engages in acceptable sex role behaviors as previously determined by student and teacher and checked off when met consistently by child, e.g.: • Male student approaches female student without placing hands on female. • Male exhibits appropriate playground behavior.

Problem Area 1D: Student engages in inappropriate activities that are biologically rooted and manifested.

Common Descriptors of this Problem Area:

- reactions to allergies, food additives
- poor coordination
- sensori-motor problems
- complaints of physical ailments (psychosomatic or real)
- listless
- tired
- vision and/or hearing problems
- organic hyperactivity
- speech problems (echolalia or stuttering)

Objectives	Activities	Evaluation
1. Student will engage in activities designed to improve motoric skills.	1. a. There are many good perceptual motor programs on the market. These include the DLM materials, Frostig materials, Getman materials, and Kephart-based activities. Although there is a great deal of debate as to the effectiveness of these activities, most people are generally agreed that their effectiveness is greater with younger children (under 8). b. Adaptive PE is a must for a student with physical problems. c. An excellent source of physical games for learning is Bryant Cratty's *Active Learning: Games to Enhance Academic Abilities.*	1. Motoric activities usually have skill level attainment measures for evaluation included. Simply include them in your IEP.
2. Student will demonstrate improved self-care skills. 3. Student will become aware of his physical delimitations and will strive towards an accepting attitude.	2-3. In the area of self-care, if the teacher should need a guide beyond what she could develop herself, two good sources are Tawney's *Programmed Environments Curriculum* and Bender's *Teaching the Moderately & Severely Handicapped*, Vols. 1, 2, and 3. Dealing with one's acceptance of physical delimitations is a nebulous endeavor. One approach might be to talk about famous persons with obvious delimitations, i.e. Helen Keller, Franklin Roosevelt, etc., and how they overcame them. The teacher could also arrange for visitors with handicaps to talk to the class about how they have compensated for their disability. Then the student(s) could talk individually or as a class about dealing with their own problem. Here again, give the student time to find and develop a skill unique to him.	2. Self-care skills are usually task analyzed and evaluated by checking off date of skill attainment, e.g. Student is toilet trained: date achieved _____ 3. Acceptance of physical delimitation is gradually arrived at if it ever really is, however, student does need to be aware of his limitation and needs the teacher's help in moving towards that acceptance.

4. Student will learn importance of controlling diet in relation to food additives and allergenic foods.

4. a. Student can do scientific experiments under the teacher's guidance to study the various effects on mice and men of caffeine, food additives, and sugar. In conjunction, students could arrange for visits to the class of the school dietician, county health nurse, or a doctor.

 b. Make comparison studies among different races and age groups of their diets and health.

 c. If a student eats a great deal of sugar foods and has "hyperactive" behavior discuss with parents the possibility of the child getting a glucose-tolerance test. Many hyperactive children are really reacting to the sugar content in their system.

4. Student scores _____ % on test to measure knowledge of unit on _____ (drugs, additives, preservations, stimulants, sugar, etc.).

5. Student is aware of the effect of his emotional state on his speech, i.e. rapid, short, choppy, stuttering, and echolalia.

5. If the student is unable to admit or recognize the variance in his speech, record them on a tape player and then sit down and discuss his speech and how he might catch himself when he recognizes a change in his speech.

5. Student consciously controls voice in stressful situation and records such control in log which is reviewed periodically by teacher.

GOAL 2: IMPROVED INTRAPERSONAL COMMUNICATION SKILLS

Definition: Characterized by personal feelings, feelings of self-worth, actions directed towards self, having inappropriate thought patterns, yet does not necessarily require another person to be present to occur.

Problem Area 2A: Inappropriate perceptions of one's feelings.

Common Descriptors of this Problem Area:

- unwarranted or uncontrolled anxiety
- inappropriate beliefs
- poorly defined values system
- moody
- apathetic
- self-derogatory
- no self-confidence
- poor self-awareness
- lack of pride
- cannot express/recognize feelings
- overly sensitive
- fantasizes excessively
- silly
- immature

Objectives	Activities	Evaluation
1. Student will successfully differentiate between constructive and destructive emotions.	1-5.	1-5.
2. Student will sucessfully recognize effects of various emotional states on his behavior.	a. PREP materials by Arista Corp. are excellent for this. Additionally, teachers can develop daily mini-lessons on security, confidence, independence, values, sad–glad–mad, love–death, pride, "I"ness, "we"ness, trust, personal satisfaction of jobs well done, and achievement. Examples of destructive emotions: silliness, immaturity, anger, jealousy, anxiety, apathy/ indifference, withdrawal, and pettiness.	a. The teacher, unannounced, stops the class, asks Johnny to describe how he is feeling, then checks that against how she sees him (or she could include the class opinion) - Do they match?
3. Student can accurately describe his present emotional state.		b. Student demonstrates by his actions that ____% of time during the day he is engaging in constructive emotions. This is supported by teacher or child observation or tabulation.
4. Student feels secure enough to share his emotions with others.	b. Use DUSO Kits.	c. Student ____% of time accurately describes emotional state of teacher, or classmates.
5. Student recognizes the effect his emotional state has on others.	c. Teacher introduces the concept of non-verbal cues and how to read them; students role play interpreting different emotions, or they can interview each other on how various emotions effect their behavior. Students can keep logs of how they feel and correspondingly act during the entire day. Have the whole class learn to "read" a student to show how consistent he is or how he is seen by others. Also compare this to how he sees himself.	d. Student articulates what constitutes security for him/her.
		e. Student verbalizes effect of his behavior on others.
		f. When asked to analyze the events of a just concluded disruptive episode, student's perceptions correctly match those of the teacher's and a majority of student's involved.

Problem Area 2B: Inappropriate perceptions of one's body.

Common Descriptors of
this Problem Area:
- no self-concept of body
- cannot relax
- masturbation
- self-mutilation
- does not trust his own body
- undefined sense of his own
- sexuality
- exhibitionism

Objectives	Activities	Evaluation
1. Student demonstrates a positive awareness of his body.	Under this heading, rather than list activities related to each objective, a listing of concepts to be covered are included. The teacher's imagination would be required to implement specifics.	1–4.
2. Student explores relationship between his body and his emotions and their effect on each other.	1 Activities related to body awareness could center around the concepts of acceptance, function, pride, enjoyment of and trusting in one's body.	a. Students will score _____ % accuracy on tests that measure mastery of the concept(s) of
3. Student is able to explain relationship of his body and sexuality.	2 Activities related to the relationship between body and emotions might include teaching the use of leisure time, relaxation therapy techniques, biofeedback, facets of psychosomatic illnesses, effects and the releasing of tension, and persistent body complaints.	b. Student is able to verbalize an acceptable perception of his sexuality and demonstrates the perception accordingly in teacher-observed settings.
4. Student develops values necessary for caring for his body.	3 Activities related to sexuality could include discussions of masturbation, exhibitionism, sex role expectations, role models, love, feelings, infatuation, marriage, dating, and children, best handled one-on-one, and with principal's awareness.	
	4 Activities related to self-care skills. In teaching traditional self-care skills (see 1D activities) include discussions or reports or activities around common abuses to the body such as drugs, self-mutilation, strain, fatigue, exercise, diet, and food additives. Activities could follow a scientific inquiry approach, and the students can do surveys and studies in these areas. Films or lecturers are also available from the Red Cross, Mental Health Associations, Public Libraries, and Regional Health Departments.	

Problem Area 2C:
Common Descriptors of
this Problem Area: Inappropriate perceptions of one's coping skills.

- maladaptive behavior
- poor reasoning ability
- illogical thinking
- irrational thoughts
- falls apart under stress
- pessimistic
- lack of independence
- no personal flexibility
- poor management skills
- poor problem solving skills
- inadequate decision making skills
- has limited options
- unrealistic expectations
- not reality oriented
- non-assertive
- does not accept failure

Objectives	Activities	Evaluation
1. Student can articulate relationship between coping skills and adaptive behavior.	1. a. Activities related to coping skills might include asking "what are" coping skills, does everyone have them, why have them, what is adaptive behavior, can different people have different coping skills? b. Do studies or surveys on how different students cope with failure, fear, school, friends, enemies, parents, cheating, frustration, etc. c. Present common problematic situations and have students relate how they would cope with the problem, and how their parents or teachers or friends might cope with the same problem. d. How do coping skills develop? Discuss the effects of experiences and personal perceptions on the development of coping skills. e. Role play "expected" coping skills of kids vs. parents, boys vs. girls, blacks vs. whites vs. other minorities, teachers vs. students, etc.	1. The best way to evaluate coping skills is to see them in action, so present role-play situations, do simulations, create crises, do natural observation of the student at free-time or in other classes, or tabulate frequency of utilization of inadequate coping skills and note their rate of decrease and the increase of adaptive coping skills. Since the student is not going to *suddenly* arrive at acceptable coping skills, or is not going to consistently apply them, evaluation will sometimes be indirect as in the decrease in the number of times of his use of inadequate coping skills.
2. Student can articulate effect of emotions of one's coping skills.	2. What are and how do we develop optimism, assertiveness, reality orientation, dealing with failure or success, and skills to keep from falling apart under stress.	2. Some sample evaluations might include: a. When Paula enters a new situation she does not react by blurting out expletives, or b. When confronted with his misbehavior Joey will not deny his actions, or

c. When classroom arrangement is changed the student accepts the change and finds his materials, or
d. When the teacher creates a mock-problem situation the student resolves the conflict appropriately.

3. Student demonstrates objective analysis of life's problem's and enacts steps to prevent their repeated occurrence.
4. Student thoroughly explores his options before making decisions (see Chapter 3).
5. Student will strive to accept his ability level and feel secure in it.

3-5

a. Find games and tasks in the class, school, or community that teach, stress, and practice logical thinking, analysis, synthesis, gathering information, developing reasoning abilities, management skills, and learning from mistakes, and relate all of the aforementioned to solving personal problems.

b. Games are excellent at teaching these concepts as long as the teacher reviews and gets the students to articulate what the goal was that the game was trying to achieve.

c. Play cards, the stock market, do scavenger hunts, teach chess, backgammon, othello, or TWIXT, play mathematical games, do mind teasers, do hidden word and crossword puzzles, discuss TV soaps or show situations, read newspapers, discuss crimes and how they might have been prevented, but above all impress upon the student the need to transfer game skill to life skills in which he assumes the responsibility for his life.

Problem Area 2D: **Inappropriate perceptions of one's social responsibilities.**
Common Descriptors of
    this Problem Area: ● no sense of obligation
               ● cannot assume responsibility for personal
                 organization, actions, or behavior
               ● cannot conform to limits

Objectives	Activities	Evaluation
1. Student will correctly differentiate between meeting societal demands and maintaining personal integrity as they effect his ability to assume responsibilities. 2. Student demonstrates his ability to assume responsibility for himself and his actions. 3. Student is able to assume his responsibility to larger society by practicing adaptive conformity.	1-3. a. All three objectives can be thoroughly covered and inculcated in any age student by discussing the mechanics of transactional analysis. Topics that might be covered would be the parent-adult-child (P-A-C) personality states, scripting, and games. Students might learn the theory then apply TA to hypothetical situations first, to their age group next, and finally to themselves. b. Additionally, examine the need for rules in society, how to make or change rules, what constitutes conformity, and how one acts in different settings.	1-3. a. Student will define with _____ % accuracy the following terms. (Teacher lists selected TA terminology.) b. Student will correctly script with _____ % accuracy 4 of 6 given conflict-producing situations. c. Student will correctly name the TA game in progress in teacher-directed role plays with a _____ % rate of accuracy. d. Student will articulate at least _____ personal values dear to him and define their relationship with his parent's, friend's, and teacher's values.

Problem Area 2E: Inappropriate perceptions of others and the environment.

Common Descriptors of
this Problem Area:
- lack of trust
- no respect for authority, adults, peers or property
- no sense of fair play
- avoids adults
- little empathy
- open defiance
- inappropriate concept of love and death

Objectives	Activities	Evaluation

1. Student can cope with other's feelings towards him.
2. Student learns how to deal with rejection and unreliable individuals.
3. Student demonstrates ability to discriminatively trust others and environment.
4. Student can articulate how he sees others coping with their problems.
	1-4.
	a. In helping children deal with others, the teacher must first establish with the child that he is OK. He should also understand that many times we take rejection as a personal affront to ourselves and as proof that we are not OK. As he has fears, concerns, insecurities, inadequacies, and short comings, so too do others. The task is not to take it all personally. Also important in this discussion would be a discussion of trust, what it is, how it is earned, and how it should be treated. Many children learn early on not to trust anyone. The teacher's goal is to help the child see that all he has to do is find just one adult that he can trust, because if he can find just one, then there must be others. This is the basis of hope and personal optimism.
	b. As activities, projects could be initiated to study motivation and how it moves people to behave appropriately or inappropriately. The teacher and student can explore different roles and corresponding role expectations, and what to do if rejected.
	c. Other activities could revolve around the following works:
	Thomas Gordon's
	    Parent Effectiveness Training (PET) or
	    Teacher Effectiveness Training (TET)
	Wayne Dyar's
	    Your Erroneous Zones or *Pulling Your Own Strings*
	McDonald's
	    Guilt-free
	d. Another activity would be to teach students the use of non-verbal messages in establishing and reading trust in others.
		1-4.
		Here, again, a student does not just "arrive" at trust, he moves towards it. Indications that he is moving might be:
		• Does he warm up to any particular adult in his environment?
		• Does he tell any adult facts that are deep, dark secrets?
		• Does he want to spend increasing amounts of time with a particular adult in his world?
		• If he has a confrontation with an adult, is he able to objectively analyze the transaction, place blame accordingly, and articulate the possible motives of the adult in doing whatever transpired?
		• Do his verbalizations place less blame on others in terms of denial of his involvement in his problem.

GOAL 3: IMPROVED INTERPERSONAL COMMUNICATION SKILLS

Definition: Characterized by verbal/non-verbal communication with others or the environment. Includes expression of thoughts and typically requires an additional person to be present to occur.

Problem Area 3A: Student is not receiving communication from the environment.

Common Descriptors of this Problem Area:
- no listening skills (readiness to receive)
- no attending skills
- cannot read body language of others
- does not acknowledge instruction or commands

Objectives	Activities	Evaluation
1. Student exhibits non-verbal cues indicative of his readiness to engage in listening activities. 2. Student can initiate and sustain appropriate listening skills. 3. Student recognizes and successfully interprets non-verbal messages from others.	1-3. a. There are many listening skill development activities available to the teacher. DLM is probably the best known producer of auditory discrimination activities. Additionally, the teacher can devise games in class to develop different skills, e.g. listening to pop records and picking out the different instruments, or having the entire class talk at the same time and then ask one student to listen to what another student is saying specifically and then share with the class how much he actually heard. Have students whisper a saying or phrase in someone else's ear, passing it on, and seeing how it comes out in the end. b. Teachers can initiate discussions on non-verbal communications and then have students pantomime guessing each others feelings, or play games like body-talk, all of which are designed to help the child read other people. c. Students can send messages to each other non-verbally or try to read one person and see how accurate everyone is. d. Have students listen to a message or a tape player with assorted distractions to see who can get the most of the message.	1-3. a. Student will demonstrate correct listening posture and actions communicated non-verbally to the teacher. b. Under test conditions, with classroom distractions, student will successfully repeat back teacher-administered instructions over_____ trials with_____ accuracy. c. Student will carry a tally sheet to be signed by his regular classroom teachers when he demonstrates appropriate listening skills in his classes. When student receives_____ signatures within_____ days/weeks/classes/etc., this goal will be met. d. Student will successfully identify the non-verbal messages of the teacher in a simulation exercise with_____ % accuracy.

Problem Area 3B: Student is not comprehending communication attempts.

Common Descriptors of
this Problem Area:
- no acknowledgement of communication
- cannot recognize needs of others
- cannot comprehend concept of or need for compromise
- cannot negotiate

Objectives	Activities	Evaluation
1. Student verbally or physically acknowledges receipt of outside communication. 2. Student comprehends that others in his world have needs and is able to correctly identify them. 3. Student accepts the need for and engages in consensus reaching (compromise) in communication.	3B. Activities and Evaluation (See activities under 2C, 3A, and 3C.) 1-3. These objectives are partially covered under other objectives. They are included here separately because in developing communication skills the usually accepted analysis of communication involves reception (3A), association (3B), and expression (3C). However, it is very difficult to factorially distinguish between association (or comprehension) and expression skills. Yet, association activities need to be acknowledged under a structured, orderly framework as an important and a necessary function, and as such are done so here.	

Problem Area 3C: Student does not respond appropriately to outside communication.

Common Descriptors of this Problem Area:

- does not make needs known appropriately
- does not communicate appropriate body language (evidenced by: defensive stance, mismatch between words expressed and feeling(s) communicated, response to being touched, and lack of eye contact)
- inappropriate response
- bizarre language content
- talks excessively
- swearing
- lies
- sex talk
- exaggerates
- argues
- name calling
- perseveration
- parrotting
- echolalia
- odd noises
- complains

Objectives	Activities	Evaluation
1. Student will accurately express thoughts and feelings in words to others. 2. Student will respond to others in the environment using socially acceptable and expected language and responses. 3. Student will engage less in non-meaningful or non-productive speech and language. 4. Student will become aware of the effect of his non-verbal expressions on others. 5. Student will appropriately use his body language to communicate thoughts and ideas.	1-5. a. Teacher asks student to express in words how various emotions makes one feel, i.e. mad, glad, sad. b. Teacher identifies (recognizes) various moods in student, stops him, and asks him to put into words how he is feeling right now. c. Teacher, in role-play situation, asks students to work through feelings of frustration, anger, glad, etc. d. Teacher and students write plays dealing with commonly occurring problems. (Duso Kits are good for this.) e. Teacher establishes situations where different students respond to the same problem in different ways — either non-accepting, gruff, or cursing, and then discusses the effects on the student of his response (verbal and non-verbal) and his eventual solution to the problem. f. Teacher sets contingencies to encourage appropriate response patterns by students to given situations. g. Teacher demonstrates different ways to respond, showing the student his options and then the class practices together. Talley sheets can be kept to record how many times student responds in new response and old response patterns. h. Teacher ignores inappropriate verbalizations of single student and gets the class to help by rewarding them. i. See 3A, non-verbal activities.	1-5. a. Teacher scores student on simulation test where he expresses his feelings in words. b. Student will keep a signed log of instances where acceptable and unacceptable alternatives were expressed. The goal is to get the unacceptable percent down below the acceptable. c. Teacher assesses student's verbal and non-verbal messages for congruence. As they approach congruence goal is said to have been attained.

Chapter 3

ACHIEVING ADAPTIVE BEHAVIOR

As potentially useful as the CRC might be, if not implemented properly, the best it can hope to achieve is mediocrity. What the CRC needs to insure its success is to be implemented with the "right" understanding of the philosophy underlying its conceptualization. The CRC is a response to a need that was evident from many years of teaching, observations, and discussions with other teachers. A previously unstated goal of the CRC was to provide the EC teacher with the structure and support to help the EC child achieve adaptive behavior. Adaptive behavior, as defined earlier, exists when the individual's coping skills and personal values are equal to or greater than the demands placed on that individual by the environment and society's values. Any individual must have personal values or beliefs that serve as his anchor in times of conflict. Too, how he copes with stress or conflict determines his own coping skills. Yet, from time to time, the environment places undue demands on us, or society's constantly changing values cause us to question our own values. At this time we are experiencing conflict and if untended can manifest itself as maladaptive behavior.

The teacher, therapist, friend, or parent's desire is to help the individual become adaptive again. How they go about rendering that aid determines in great measure the degree of success the individual in conflict will enjoy. One of the first rules to remember is that no one can make someone else learn, behave, or be adaptive. That decision ultimately rests with the person in conflict. The goal of the intervention is to facilitate as much as possible the making of that decision by the EC child. There are many considerations to be made in attempting to facilitate adaptive behavior on the part of another. Those considerations can be loosely grouped into three categories: (1) personality factors of the teacher, (2) positive intervention techniques, and (3) potential pitfalls. All three should be kept in mind by the teacher in planning the child's IEP based upon the CRC.

INFLUENCE OF TEACHER PERSONALITY

The teacher's personality is the one driving force behind most successful interventions with conflicted children. Teacher personality is the most elusive yet most potentially effective tool the teacher has. A majority of teachers overlook this fact and are doomed to a career of frustration, anxiety, and nonfulfillment. Many teachers hide behind techniques, so that when they fail they can put the blame on the technique and not on themselves.

The personality factor applied to intervention with EC children can take four forms. These forms depict the mental "set" from which the teacher approaches his job. These sets or philosophies are *babysitting* vs. *control* vs. *parenting* vs. *modeling*. The teacher is frequently not even aware that he is following a particular philosophy.

The teacher that adopts a *babysitting* stance takes the path of least resistance. There are no demands placed on the children to perform or meet any levels of competence. These are merely unfortunate children that have had a bad enough life already and do not need any more problems. They are given lots of freedom and encouraged to engage in "fun" activities. The teacher typically makes statements about how he just "loves" the children. The goal is a pressure-free environment where children can feel safe. The children usually dictate to the teacher what they want, and there is no direction or structure in the class. What results from this approach borders on anarchy. There is no semblance of order, and the children certainly do not learn how to deal realistically with their problems.

Control represents the opposite extreme of babysitting. The teacher allows no opportunities for the child to misbehave. This is really the easiest choice of the four to pursue, because the teacher literally squelches all misbehavior and does not allow it to get going, much less out of hand. Frequently teachers can be heard to exclaim that they have no discipline problems or that kids do not misbehave in their class. This is an immediate tip-off that they are probably "controlling" their class. This approach requires a constant vigil on the part of the teachers so that they might "nip in the bud" any potential problem. The teacher rules by threat, intimidation, sarcasm, and severe punishment. The teacher assumes all responsibility. This approach does not encourage divergent thinking or question asking. One result is that kids do not develop coping skills. In fact, they tend to become more disruptive in other settings in order to vent pent-up frustrations. This might also occur if the new setting is open, because the children do not have the skills to deal with an open environment. The real learning that emerges from the "control" setting is a good lesson in adult power. What the teacher is communicating to the child is that, "I am bigger, meaner, and stronger then you. You have no say-so, and when you get big, then you can act just like me," which is exactly what many students do when they grow up.

The third approach is *parenting*. This approach stimulates various reactions. They may be positive or negative, but this approach generally connotes lots of love given by the teacher to the child. The teacher treats the child as he does or would his own. The teacher guides and directs the child, helps them when they stumble, and provides support and solace for the child when needed. The responsibility for student growth is a shared responsibility between teacher and child. This approach is generally good and usually effective. The only pitfall is that teachers cannot take the place of real parents. And the real parents whether good or bad, present at home or not, will always occupy the highest spot in the child's perceptions of the real world. A child's parent(s) could be absolutely and unequivocally inadequate, and the child would still stand by them. After all, they are the only parent(s) the child has. Like the once popular song says, "Even a bad love is better than no love at all." It is very difficult to get EC children to objectively see the nature of their relationships with their parent(s).

Almost without exception, the EC children that I have encountered over the years have automatically assumed themselves to be at fault for not being "OK" or not being able to get along with their folks at home. Children have great difficulty in accepting that they might really be OK, and that they are merely a pawn that is being manipulated by a maladaptive parent. For this reason, as potentially powerful as parenting is as a philosophy to adopt in working with EC children, it will never allow the teacher to completely substitute for the "real thing." Additionally, it presents a very tenuous subject to broach with the child. As soon as attempts are made by the teacher to help the child see his role in the parent-offspring relationship, the child goes home telling the parent that the teacher said that the parent is "bad," then the teacher really has problems.

The fourth choice is *modeling*. Modeling is the most talked about of the four choices. Its proponents advocate modeling as the only real alternative to long-lasting intervention. As it does appear to be the best tool for use with many EC children, modeling gets discussed frequently, but to what degree does it really get utilized? The answer is that modeling is used all of the time by adults and the children around them. The problem is that teachers are oftentimes unaware that they are modeling certain behavior patterns, and, as is frequently the case, the modeling has a negative effect upon the intended.

Argyris and Schön (1974) have provided very realistic means by which to examine this phenomenon of unawares modeling. The domain under discussion is called *action theories*. Action theories are examined in two units, espoused theories and in-use theories. Espoused theories of action are those beliefs, values, and fundamental axioms that teachers say they believe in and operate by. For instance, in EC intervention many teachers/therapists espouse a personal style of operating that is founded upon the precepts of learning theory. They believe in learning theory and in the procedures derived from learning theory, i.e. behavior modification. To them, the notion of environmental precipitors to behavior, unemotional involvement on the part of the teacher/therapist in changing that behavior, the lack of concern for the why of specific behaviors, the collection of baseline, intervention, and post-intervention data to assess effectiveness, etc., is appealing, logical, and the only course to follow in changing maladaptive behaviors. These beliefs become that person's espoused theory of action, i.e. what he/she says he believes. Yet if in the course of implementing these beliefs, the person becomes more psychodynamic in nature by trying, for example, to get the student to develop some insight into the nature of his behavior, trying to get that same person to internalize and generalize certain new adaptive responses, and just generally show genuine feelings of regard for the student, then these actions constitute that teacher's in-use theory. In-use theories of action refer to what the teacher/therapist actually does in the course of his interventions.

The measure of similarity between one's espoused theories and in-use theories is called *congruence*. The amount of congruence indicates the degree of agreement between espoused and in-use. If one's espoused beliefs are in fact carried out in-use, then the congruence is said to be high, and similarly low if one's espoused beliefs differ markedly from their in-use. Congruence does not imply correctness of that theory. This is an important distinction. If a teacher exhibits a high degree of congruence, that congruence makes no statement about the correctness or effectiveness of the teacher's approach. The congruence value depicts consistency, which is important in working with EC children. An example of congruence, yet questionability of approach, is the Doman and Delacato (1966) neurological repatterning approach to the amelioration of severe learning disabilities. Parents' belief in and implementation of the techniques espoused by Doman and Delacato may yield a very high congruence, yet the techniques themselves have still to be accepted on a wide scale as valid.

Argyris and Schön (1974) state the conditions conducive to congruence as: "A behavioral world of low self-deception, high availability of feelings, and low threat is conducive to congruence; a behavioral world of low self-esteem and high threat is conducive to self-deception and incongruence" (p.23).

Congruence discussed in the realm of modeling assumes added significance. Often a teacher will espouse to using modeling techniques to effect positive change in students, when in actuality the teacher is perceived entirely different by his students. This is one indication that modeling is used positively or negatively and unknowingly by teachers. Thus, the different stances possible might be:

1. A teacher that espouses modeling and uses it effectively (high congruence, valid theory).
2. A teacher that espouses modeling and uses it ineffectively (low congruence,valid theory).
3. A teacher that does not espouse modeling, but uses it effectively (low congruence because what they say they believe, i.e. disbelief in modeling and what they do are incongruent, and invalid theory, i.e. disbelief in effectiveness of modeling).
4. A teacher that does not espouse modeling and uses it ineffectively (high congruence, invalid theory).

Of the four choices one and three are best, while two and four are not. Teacher three is the "natural" teacher. He/she intuitively practices adaptive techniques. There are not many "natural" teachers, but most teachers can be effective by practicing stance one conscientiously. And hopefully by raising the level of consciousness of teachers two and four towards modeling, they will become more effective teachers.

An indirect method exists for discussing modeling, and that is how adults, whether they admit it or not, have modeled from others in their environment. Think back to your favorite teachers, friends, or adults when you were growing up. What do you remember most about them? Were they tough, fair, or just acknowledged you as an individual? Did you say or think that when you grew up you wanted to be just like them? This is modeling. There is some thought that as adults we select careers, friends, and values that complement our personalities (Newcomb, 1974). These values are formulated over time and via modeling. The statement is frequently made that teachers teach as they were taught, or parents parent as they were parented. These statements are generally true and are indicative of the sheer power of modeling. It is indicative too of the fact that modeling occurs whether one is aware of it or not. The question becomes that if modeling is significant in shaping behavior, then can it not be applied consciously and methodically to effect positive growth in all children, and particularly with EC children? If children are going to shop around among adults and pick and choose from the styles they see forthcoming, why not maximize on it? Why not let those same students see how we as teachers approach conflicts, solve problems, make decisions, and cope? Maybe they will like what they see and emulate their teachers; in so doing they will have taken a big step towards achieving adaptive behavior.

Modeling can be used advantageously or nonadvantageously. Kids do not shop from "perfect" teachers. Perfect teachers are ones that never make or admit to mistakes. They hide behind brick walls and do not get involved with students. Students know that they themselves make mistakes and, therefore, know they could never be like their perfect teacher. The perfect teacher models unrealistic and unattainable behaviors and is, hence, a negative model. Another variety of a negative model is one whose style is not considered conducive to acquiring adaptive behaviors. Putting the leader of a notorious street gang into a classroom to teach would provide the students someone they could possibly identify with but not someone that other adults would think would be a positive influence; hence, they would be a negative model.

What keeps the teacher that would like to be a Mr. Dixon (from the TV series *Room 222*) or a Lucas Tanner from being one? Do not all teachers really start out with the right intentions? Why do they have this problem of translating intentions into actions? Why are they so incongruent? The basic tenents of modeling espouse one's knowing and "accepting" one's weaknesses and strengths. The key here is the *accepting*. Teachers should examine their strengths and weaknesses. They should also know how to deal with each when confronted with a student that requires tapping that strength or weakness. Looking at ourselves critically requires a great deal of effort and can be especially painful if we do not like what we see. It is like Carl Rogers's ideal-

and real-self analogies. We may see ourselves ideally one way, but when confronted with how we really are, it may be very disquieting. To keep from finding ourselves faced with this dilemma, we all establish elaborate defense barriers around ourselves to keep others from seeing how we really feel. A man may see a movie that really touches a soft spot within, but he knows that macho men do not cry so he over reacts by putting the movie down. A teacher is asked a touchy question and shakes if off by laughing (really nervous laughter) to show that it does not bother him/her. We surround ourselves with people just like ourselves to validate ourselves. There really is security in numbers. This is the spawning ground of the single most prevalent cause of emotional conflict — racism. Regardless of how open we might be, no one takes criticism well, at least not initially. After we have thought about the criticism awhile, an open person can accept it and take it as it was hopefully intended, constructively. But at the exact moment of receipt criticism hurts. Thus, people shy away from self-analysis, because it is so potentially uncomfortable. People avoid unpleasantness. The end result is everybody becomes adept at rationalization. Ever notice that if someone wants something bad enough, that person can rationalize reasons for going ahead and getting it? Consequently, whatever our strengths and weaknesses, we can find assorted means to rationalize ourselves and our "OK'ness." This is human nature.

Teachers can overcome these inherent problems and can be positive models. If students learn by modeling, and it can be assumed they do, then teachers ought to feel compelled to capitalize on modeling as an additional tool. If one aspires to be an effective model, what kinds of factors should he be cognizant of?

Rule one is to feel good about who you are and what you are. Accept yourself as you are and build or improve on that as you see appropriate. It really is OK to admit to yourself and publicly that you have shortcomings. If a child asks a question you cannot answer, simply say, "You know, I just do not know, but let's find out together!" This one statement alone will do more towards developing trust and credibility with students than anything else a teacher could say. Required, too, is a certain amount of wanting to please others, of being thoughtful and considerate towards others, and simply just caring. Again, just the adoption of these ideals is tremendously effective.

Getting into a positive role model might be harder initially, but once there it is easier to maintain than its alternatives. It is harder to get into because it sometimes requires "bucking the system" to pursue something for a child or yourself that you really believe in. Harder, too, because what people really want out of life is security however one defines security, i.e. family, home, money, friends, prestige, and one does not always feel secure marching to the beat of a different drummer (Thoreau). The biggest reason is the risk taking that is required to be a positive model, not life-threatening risks, but security-threatening ones. Once a person establishes himself in a secure perspective or position, he becomes less inclined to take risks. He does not want to rock the boat or jeopardize his position or accomplishments. This course of non-risk-taking leads directly and inevitably to complacency. Complacency is synonymous with stagnation and results in decreased efficiency, which in the area of EC intervention equates to less effectiveness at imparting adaptive skills to the students that need them the most. When we are "different" we run the risk of not being accepted, and acceptance is critically important to all of us, regardless of how open and together we might see ourselves as being. But being "different" is again the one factor that makes us more credible to the EC child. He knows all too well that he is different. If he perceives his teacher as being different, then he says, "this is attainable." This underscores the development of the trust that is the prerequisite to helping a child learn adaptive behaviors.

Once you accept these precepts to modeling and earnestly pursue and use them, it becomes easier to maintain the new positive stance than the old closed ones. There are several guides to keep in mind when adopting and maintaining a positive modeling position. I feel strongly about everything written in this book, but I feel strongest about the following axioms of modeling. *They work and will continue to work if applied sincerely, honestly, and all the time.*

1. ASSUME AN ADAPTIVE STANCE AND BE FLEXIBLE. This is a constant process of asking yourself, "What have I learned and how can I apply it to improve myself?"
2. MAINTAIN YOUR PERSPECTIVE. Do not spin your wheels or expend wasted energy trying to change things that cannot be changed. Decide what can be changed and pursue that. More satisfaction can and will be derived by pursuing realistic goals than attempting unattainable ones.
3. TAKE RISKS. People with adaptive life-styles take chances, not reckless ones, but calculated ones designed to attain predetermined goals. Risk taking keeps all your skills in tune.
4. KEEP A SENSE OF HUMOR. Be able to laugh at yourself, and with others, and be able to enjoy life's humorous moments. Never take yourself too seriously, because then you become pompous and lose your effectiveness as a teacher. Oftentimes a sense of humor is the only thing that can get you through a particularly tough day with EC children. When the job ceases to be fun, get out!
5. THERE IS ALWAYS A BETTER WAY TO DO THINGS. There is no one way to do anything. Most of the creative things ever done were in response to looking for a better way to get a job done. This is also true in behavior disorders. There are better ways to help kids and it's up to us, not someone else, to find them.
6. BE FAIR. Put yourself into the shoes of the child you are working with. Ask yourself, "If I were in his position, listening to what I am saying or doing, would I buy it?" If not, then you should not do it. It is better to let him get away with it this time if you are not sure than to punish him

wrongly. He will present other opportunities where you will know you are right in pursuing whatever course you elect.

7. YOU HAVE GOT TO BELIEVE IN YOUR APPROACH. You have got to believe that you are right. This gives you confidence that the child picks up on and subsequently believes in too. Many teachers fail in their attempts to work with EC children because they just do not believe in the techniques they are using. They will adopt a course of action that subconsciously they do not support and which inevitably will fail.

8. BE A GOOD LISTENER. The world is full of people who feel the need to talk to impress others that they are OK. Be comfortable enough with yourself to know that you do not need to impress others with words. You will impress them with your actions. This will free you to listen to others.

9. MAKE THE FIRST MOVE. Initiate action. Someone has to, why not you? It will never get done otherwise.

10. LEARN AND PRACTICE THE DIFFERENCE BETWEEN ASSERTIVENESS AND AGGRESSIVENESS. Assertiveness means standing up for yourself, striving towards self-actualization, and getting your needs met. It does not mean being hostile, infringing on other's rights, hurting others, or in short, aggressively threatening others.

Ten simple rules, easy to list and agree to; very hard to implement without constant attention. Bad habits do not go away by themselves. Likewise new ones do not just appear. They require diligent effort to implant. We often hear new or good ideas and say to ourselves, "I am going to start doing that." But unless it is thought of repeatedly, it is soon forgotten. It is the many-mini approach advocated in Chapter 2 applied to our own personal lives. This entire section can be concluded by noting what a good leader is. A good leader is one that when the job is done, everyone involved feels they are the one that made it successful.

POSITIVE INTERVENTION TECHNIQUES

When techniques for intervention with EC children are discussed, certain recurring ones are mentioned. Techniques like planned ignoring, reinforcement, counter-conditioning, self-analysis, counseling, contingency management, satiation, and more recently, relaxation therapy are given considerable review in the literature on intervention with EC children (Hewett and Taylor, 1980; Kauffman, 1977; Reinert, 1976; Shea, 1978). Most teachers routinely include such techniques in their repetoire of skills. There exists, however, another level or area of techniques or skills that are not as routinely discussed or employed.

The use of these skills is one of the major factors distinguishing the best teachers from the merely adequate ones. A lot is said about learning style, but what about adaptive style? The mark of really good teachers is the adaptive style in which they help children learn to cope. The influence of the teacher's personality on this style has already been previously discussed. Another facet of this adaptive style is the level of techniques they employ. Most of the techniques previously mentioned and generally employed by EC teachers can be taught to and employed by behavior technicians. The best and most successful teachers bring a higher degree of sophistication to task in working with EC students. This sophistication is part of the artistry of effective teaching. Whenever one attempts to dissect, analyze, and make observations about that artistry, the nebulous quality is frequently lost. Words used to summarize attempts at objective analysis cannot convey the emotions or feelings that are applied to effective intervention. So we grasp with ways to assess effective teaching. Herein, then, is another attempt.

I am convinced that what makes teachers really effective at developing adaptive behaviors in children in conflict is their unique abilities to impart to the child the single fact that he has options that he can pursue to make decisions about his behavior. The EC child has traditionally had few, if any, options

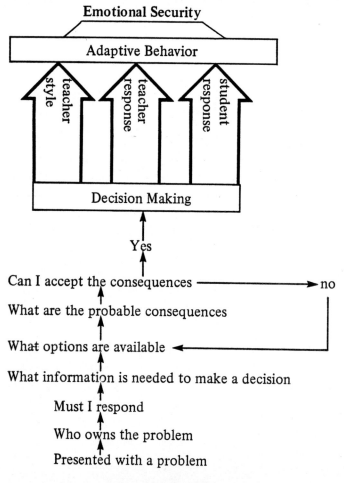

Figure 3-1. Decision-Making Paradigm (Emotional Security.)

available to him — not options in terms of service alternatives, but options in terms of response modes to his maladaptive behaviors. All he has been able to do is lash out or withdraw. Good teachers will show him his choices to this fight-or-flight syndrome. Figure 3-1 will help us examine this issue.

Emotional security is the ultimate goal towards which we all strive. It may only be an ideal, but an ideal nonetheless that we should all attempt to achieve. Attaining this security rests in part on the degree of adaptive behavior manifested by each individual. Which level of adaptive behavior we operate from depends upon the number of options available to us and how we use them. There are different kinds of options and different paths to follow in reaching adaptive behavior. Teacher style, teacher response, and student response are all influenced by the choices or decisions that we make. The quality or adequacy of personal decisions is based on the options available to us and how they are used in the decision-making process.

Decision making is an integral part of EC intervention. Decisions are made constantly by all parties involved. They also reflect the ultimate goal of intervention: making appropriate decisions resulting in adaptive behavior. Three different kinds of decisions must be made: those affecting teacher style, those affecting how teachers respond to students, and those decisions students must make about their own behaviors.

Positive Intervention: Teacher Style

Teacher decisions involve decisions of style. Is the teacher going to be open, firm, authoritarian, autocratic, dictatorial, etc.? I am reinforced by observations of teachers that many teachers do not consciously predetermine their style, they evolve into it as they acquire teaching experience. Even with experience, a significant number of teachers still have not recognized the impact that their teaching style has on the classroom environment. Others are aware of their style but make no attempts to improve themselves. Teaching has ceased to be fun and rewarding for an alarming number of teachers, but economics and job convenience keep them on the job. Why has it ceased to be an enjoyable vocation? Teachers are quick to point to students as the cause. The teachers say lack of motivation and discipline. The administrators blame parents and society, and the students blame teachers and administrators as uncaring and unresponsive. And everybody is partially correct. What can the uninspired teacher do?

The teacher can do at least three things: (1) she can quit spinning her wheels or wasting energy complaining about things that she has no influence over and cannot change; (2) she can stop accepting the entire responsibility for her students' behaviors; and (3) she can make a decision that she is going to start having fun teaching. This sounds really naive and idealistic, but it is not necessarily so! Teachers should adopt a positive perspective. Another name for this is the "I'm not going to let you push my button" syndrome.

Teachers spin their wheels by complaining about matters that they themselves cannot change (e.g. unresponsive administrators and the kid's bad home environment), and by doing so they have no real responsibility to try to change the situation. More and more teachers are becoming cynics instead of critics. A cynic sees everything that is wrong around him and complains and complains, but offers no solutions. A critic sees the same problems, but rather than complain, offers positive alternatives. It is easier to say, "Well, no wonder he misbehaves, look what kind of home life he has. He will not change!" With this statement the teacher has divested herself of any responsibility for failing to help the child when he continues to misbehave, which given the teacher's attitude, he will surely continue to do. Instead, the teacher should assume the role of critic and take a positive position. Her thoughts could just as easily be, "Well, maybe he does have a rotten home and does not trust adults. I can at least provide a secure, supportive environment at school and, in so doing, show him that here, at least, is one adult that he can trust. And, if he can find one, then there must be others."

While there are many contributing factors, part of the reason teachers fall into this negative cynic role is misplaced guilt. If a child is acting up in the classroom the exact instant the principal walks by, or if the class is particularly noisy in the hall, lunchroom, or school-wide assembly, then the teacher is embarrassed and feels guilty for not having done her "job." Too, if a child does have emotional conflicts, then is it not the teacher's job to show him how to cope to make him behave? When this does not happen, teachers feel guilty for failing. Should the teacher protect the child from everything? The teacher's real function is to present the child with options, to provide support in exercising those options and an environment and structure in which to experience them. Her role is not to live the child's life for him. Teachers need to get over the notion that they are at fault or personally liable for all the misbehaviors of their students. Granted, the distinction being made here is not always a clear one. Shea's (1978) statement that "no one ever told you that teaching kids like me was going to be easy" is very appropriate. The path of shared responsibility is fuzzy and results in teachers assuming and demanding of others too much responsibility from time to time. On the one side, the teacher does have a responsibility to help the EC child, and on the other side, it is not her responsibility to personally accept all of his failures and misbehaviors. She is to guide, support, and walk with the troubled child, but she also has to help him learn to stand on his own feet and ultimately accept the responsibility for his own failures and their correction.

Having fun is the issue. Not fun as in going to a party fun, but the deep personal satisfaction sort of fun derived from knowing that your professional priorities are in perspective and you are the most effective person you can be. Part of this is being truly convinced that if not for your help there would be no help for these EC children. You are their rock and security. Together with your guidance and their effort, they will make progress. This sort of satisfaction derives from personal confidence, a positive attitude, and an adaptive life-style.

Why is teaching not fun for so many teachers? Teaching ceases to be fun when teachers allow themselves to be entrapped by the manipulations of their students. Students are adept in finding ways to get to teachers. When the teacher falls prey to the student's designs, then the child's perception of chaos in his world is reinforced. Another perspective of the child's ability to create chaos is that it reflects the degree of power that a child feels he has. To create chaos successfully or manipulate others gives a child a sense of power. In the absence of other more traditional reinforcers of self-worth, e.g. parental love, school success, and peer acceptance, the EC child validates himself by how much power he has. Getting teachers upset and out of stride is very "powerful." I also call this "pushing the teacher's button." There are numerous ways to push a teacher's button, as evidenced by the following sample of student statements:

"But Miss Jones, you let Timmy do that, why can't I?"
"Oh Mr. Smith, Mary Lou was at your desk, while you were in the office."
"You just don't like me because I'm black."
"I had to take care of my mother and brothers and sisters yesterday, so I couldn't come to school."

Statements like these are quick to produce guilt in the teacher, then the teacher is automatically on the defensive. Teachers on the defensive do not routinely make prudent decisions. They usually become offensive and punitive. Once this happens the child has reaffirmed his belief that teachers cannot be trusted. And with no trust comes no growth. Button-pushing and chaos-creating are great diversionary tactics and are extremely taxing for the teacher. This is the biggest trap that all teachers fall into. A problem arises if it becomes a constant process, resulting in diminished teacher effectiveness. Obviously this is something that teachers should avoid, especially when working with EC students, whom they know are going to be extremely proficient at button-pushing. How does the teacher break out of this entrapment? The solution is to approach each day with the resolve and determination to not allow your students to push your button or get your goat, so to speak. Approach each situation with a matter-of-fact attitude. Students do a majority of their inappropriate activities solely to irritate the teacher. If their actions do not bother you, then there exists little or no reason for them to misbehave. If a child misbehaves, it is his decision to do so. No one makes anyone else do anything they do not want to do. If a child misbehaves, it is his decision to do so, even if you are wrong and have forced him into a limited-response situation.

When a child misbehaves, do not get upset; rather, state the child's behavior and his consequences if he persists in his actions. If he continues, then simply carry out the consequence. For instance, if Frank will not stay in his seat, you do not brow beat him into submission. When you do this, you place yourself and the student into a win-lose situation; even if you win, you have really lost because the child will have no respect for you and will not trust you. Instead, very clearly state Frank's choices: he can either sit down and behave or continue to misbehave and not earn a privilege. The choice is his, not yours. By doing this you have placed the burden of responsibility on his shoulders. Then, should he continue to misbehave, all you have to do is carry out the predetermined consequence. In this way you do not have to constantly walk around on tip toes wondering when Frank is going to get you. This approach avoids power struggles that frequently flare up between teachers and students. The teacher simply chooses not to engage in them. She tells her students that she enjoys working with students who know how to behave, and that she is not going to waste her time with those students who do not attempt to work properly. She makes it very clear that she is going to do her job, enjoy it, and not allow disruptive students to spoil her fun. In this way, she has insulated herself from the various attacks students tend to perpetrate.

This approach can only work if the teacher really believes in it. She must approach each day with the idea that her students are not going to force her into doing something she does not want to do. Also, she needs to anticipate all the actions of her students so that she will know what she is going to do if they do this or if they do that. She must believe that students behave the way they want to behave.

Positive Intervention: Teacher Response

After the decisions involving teacher style have been made, the teacher should then make the "how and what" decisions regarding his or her plans of intervention with EC children. Here teachers examine what options are open to them in working with their students. The facets of intervention discussed at the beginning of Chapter 2 become significant at this time, i.e. age of child, degree of involvement, approach, locus of control, setting, and environmental support. Beyond these, however, are additional points that the teacher should include in making decisions of teacher response.

These points will be examined from two perspectives. The first is how teachers might go about making response decisions, and the second discusses actual techniques for intervention. In making decisions about how to intervene with an EC child, the teacher should come to rely heavily on his or her ability to predict student behavior and on their ability to read and successfully interpret students' nonverbal communications. Better teachers, whether aware of it or not, are very successful at predicting student behavior and reading students' nonverbal cues. The advantage of proficiency at these two conditions is in already having decided what then to do when the child does react.

It is not really known if there is a finite universe of behaviors manifested by an EC child, or any child. There are consistent patterns of responses that most children fall into, and knowing what these patterns are prior to their being emitted by the child gives the teacher the advantage of already having decided what to do in any given situation with each child. These are not necessarily patterns that the teacher is aware of prior to the child's coming to the teacher for the very first time. The teacher might be aware of them through her behavior assessment or personal observations of the child. Too, the teacher knows that certain kinds of children are typically going to react to given situations in fairly predictable patterns. For instance, an acting-out child can generally be expected to react in an aggressive, asocial pattern (Reinert, 1976). *Forewarned is forearmed* sums this point concisely. Chaos is created when the child experiences an emotional episode, and the teacher is unprepared to react appropriately and quickly. How does the teacher become better at predicting behavior? The answer is difficult to articulate, but the basis depends upon the teacher's ability to attend to details in her environment. What are the subtle nuances each child manifests in connection with his maladaptive behavior? Teachers that study these details and are able to intuitively anticipate an outburst and learn from the details leading up to that outburst are going to be better at successfully working with the child. The teacher is constantly assessing the child's behavior and her responses to determine the degree of match between the behavior and the teacher's response.

After modeling, the most ignored tool at the disposal of the teacher is the use of nonverbal communications. Nonverbal communications can be used to predict behavior, to prevent the occurrence of inappropriate behavior, or to maintain new and more adaptive behaviors. One of the more poignant statements made in Ester Rothman's book *The Angel Inside Went Sour* (1971) was "Listen to what I mean, not to what I say." This is so true and reflects the crux of nonverbal communication. In fact, the *emotional content* of any transaction between two or more people is communicated verbally and nonverbally; the *emotional meaning* is interpreted more nonverbally than verbally (Lewis-Smith, 1977; Rankin, 1978). Mehrabian (1972) reported that the emotional impact of any message is communicated 7 percent verbally, 38 percent vocally, and 55 percent facially. Nonverbal communication is a powerful medium.

Students do not typically become instantly disruptive. Instead they send out coded messages that say, "Teacher, look out, I am about to become disruptive. Help me regain control." These nonverbal messages are clearly obvious by facial expression, gestures, body movements, and voice inflection. Yet most teachers ignore them until it becomes too late and they then have a "hot" child to deal with. A hot child is the hardest kind of child to deal with because he is no longer in a mood to listen. If the teacher had simply seen the child's looks of frustration, his toe-tapping, his tearing up of a worksheet or the breaking of a pencil, she could have interceded then and could have prevented the more serious flare-up. The teacher could have simply interacted with the child, possibly nonverbally herself, and have prevented serious complications. She could simply have called out his name, established eye contact, and winked or smiled or have walked in his general area to help him re-establish self-control. Developing expertness requires constant attention. It requires checking and rechecking the child's nonverbal messages. The teacher should ask herself, "What was this child communicating to me, and was I right in my interpretation and response?" In time then, the teacher that sensitizes herself to the nonverbal communications in her classes will find her rate of accuracy going way up with a concomitant decline in out-of-hand disruptions.

Once a teacher develops her skills at predicting behavior and using nonverbal communication to determine teacher response, other additional techniques exist that can be employed to maximize the widest possible range of options available to the teacher for use with EC children. These are techniques of intervention and go beyond the use of traditional tools that are assumed to be used by EC teachers automatically, e.g. social modeling, reinforcement, and contingency management (Stephens, 1978).

1. EMPHASIZE THE POSITIVE. This is so obvious that it should not even be mentioned. It is, however, a major stumbling block to many teachers of the disturbed. Every text that I have ever read says to positively reward appropriate behavior, yet I will frequently walk into an EC class and see teachers taking points away from children, or telling students what not to do rather than what to do, or, worse still, not rewarding appropriate behavior. It is difficult to reward appropriate behavior consistently. What we as teachers do is inadvertently fall into the trap of attending to disruptive behavior. We do this to maintain that air of control and orderliness in the classroom. When we spend more and more time attending to inappropriate behaviors, there is less time left over to attend to good behavior. After all, the child is supposed to be behaving and in so doing tends to get overlooked. The squeaky wheel gets the grease is so true in working with children in conflict. Teachers' intentions are honorable, but carrying them to fruition creates the bind. So remember to consciously reward every child every day for his good behavior, rather than pointing out his bad behavior. Design a plan that attends to and rewards the child's positive behavior. Underemphasize as much as is possible the negative behaviors the child manifests.

2. GIVE STUDENTS ATTENTION. Where adults seek security, children seek attention. By receiving attention, the child receives his strokes that convince him that he is in fact OK or adaptive. Find something to attend to with every child, every day that lets him know that you acknowledge and approve of his presence in your domain.

3. INSTILL TRUST. Trust is the cornerstone of effective intervention with EC children. Without it the teacher will get absolutely nowhere with the child. It is not an immediately available commodity, and it takes time and patience to develop. Most EC students learn very early in their lives that adults cannot be trusted. Adults say, "Trust me, come talk to me, and we will work it out

together." So, kids being as trusting in adults as they are, go to this adult, who it so happens does not have time for the child. The child is crushed, and after this process occurs repeatedly, learns that adults cannot be trusted. Now is the time that the EC teacher gets the child. What the teacher does in the early stages of the child-teacher interaction will determine later success. Will teachers do as others have before them or will they say to the child, "Look, we cannot help each other until we trust each other. It will take time to develop that trust. I will not push you into it. You will have to determine for yourself whether or not I can be trusted. For my part I want to say this. Earning your trust is very important to me. You are in my class because you have certain behavior problems (specify them). Now, I cannot make you behave, in fact I am not even going to try. That will have to be your decision. However, I will be here to help if and when you want it. It will be easier to change the things you do with my help. Together we can do it. I will do my very best to be available when you need me. If I am not, it does not mean that I do not care. I will get to you. If you decide in time that you can trust me, I will treat your trust as a very special gift and will do my very best not to let you down. OK? The point I am trying to make here is that (1) together we can work through your problems, and (2) if you can trust me, then that proves that at least one adult can be trusted. And if you find one, you can find others." This seems to me to be the best approach to follow in getting a child to trust in adults. It becomes a shared responsibility with realistic expectations on the part of both teacher and student.

4. REMEMBER THE IMPORTANCE OF HUMOR. Humor as a therapeutic tool has tremendous potential. If a potentially stressful situation can be redirected by using humor, everyone is allowed to salvage some pride. Too, when students and teachers are able to laugh about their problems, they have taken significant strides towards adaptive behavior. Crucial to the effective use of humor is the ability of the teacher to recognize problems in the early stage of the manifestation sequence. Once a student is really worked up, humor is less effective.

5. PROVIDE PHYSICAL TOUCH WHEN APPROPRIATE. Physical touch with younger (elementary grades) students has the same potential as humor. Hugging, caressing, or just tapping a student's shoulder serves many purposes. Touch shows a student he is accepted, redirects behavior, maintains the student in his present environment, and is reassuring. With older students, however, the question of sexuality, e.g. male teachers with female students, and female teachers with male students, must be taken into consideration before use.

6. DO NOT BE AFRAID TO SAY "NO." It is OK to tell EC students "no" to some of their requests. One of the aims of EC intervention is to help troubled children cope with stress. For this reason EC teachers make every effort to let EC children succeed. In so doing teachers try not to say no to the demands of

EC children. However, there will come a time in each child's progress where it is appropriate to expect him to successfully handle "no" situations. Too, it is better to experience "no" in a supportive environment instead of the regular classroom where the teacher is going to be less inclined to tolerate a reaction to her telling a child "no."

7. CHANGE ROUTINES. For much the same reasons as listed under saying no, a child needs to experience changes in routine. EC children tend not to be very flexible, and helping them adapt to changes in their daily routines, class activities, and even seating arrangements helps them to adjust to changes in the "real world."

8. PROVIDE SUPPORT SYSTEMS. Failure to provide students substantial support during and after the transition back to the classroom is where the system really fails those students that have made substantial growth. A child can come into an EC class manifesting a wide range of maladaptive behaviors. The teacher can then perform her miracles resulting in growth towards adaptive behavior. But if these changes are going to be internalized and generalized to different settings, then the child will need a support system in his natural setting until such time as those new behaviors become engrained as new habits in the child. Support systems can consist of assigning the EC child a buddy in the regular classroom to look out for him, or giving the child a monitor card that allows his regular classroom teacher to initial when he has had a good day. These cards can then be periodically checked by the EC teacher and redeemed for special privileges. Other kinds of support can consist of the EC teacher checking with the regular classroom teacher, or simply walking the EC child to his classroom. However it may be done, the goal is to provide constant support to the newly mainstreamed child until he has amply proven that he can make it on his own.

Positive Intervention: Student Response

In working with EC children, the teacher has as her highest goal each child's achievement of a higher level of adaptive behavior. The attainment of adaptive behavior is based upon improved coping skills, which in turn are developed by being able to solve problems successfully. And to solve problems one must be able to make realistic decisions. Therefore, what we teach EC children is that they do have options or choices, but they must make many decisions concerning which options to pursue. Emotionally Conflicted children become problem children because they either do not have or do not exercise the options available to them and generally react to all stress situations in the same response mode. Different children have different reactions, but each child has his unique response pattern that he uses in all situations. For example, one child may be mad at mom, or have been in a fight on the way to school, or he may have failed a test. Where an adaptive child might have reacted differently to each situation, the EC child might react by withdrawing and crying in each situation. He does this because it is the only way he knows how to react.

The teacher's goal is to broaden the student's response range. She wants to take a child that is a victim of his own inability to cope and improve his coping skills. She wants the child to learn the necessary skills to break his going around in circles, and this will give him freedom of choice over his own life, regardless of age. The way she accomplishes this is to present the decision-making paradigm, presented earlier, in the context of the child's problem. For instance, a child is constantly fighting with peers. Through observation and assessments she detects two recurring patterns in the child's behavior. First, the child would like to make friends but he does not know how to approach children without hitting them, and second, one of the other boys in the class senses his frustrations and is able to set the child off by taunting him. The child is clearly unable to change his pattern; hence, intervention is warranted. The teacher's approach might be to sit down and attempt to discuss the situation with the child. Having read what I have said about choices in teacher responses and in predicting behavior, this teacher has previously determined that the talk could go in at least three different ways. Having anticipated these choices *prior* to the conference, the teacher knows what she is going to do in each situation.

1. The child might talk and say that he wants to make friends but no one likes him, in which case the teacher would work with the child to show him different ways to approach children in a positive manner that will allow him to make friends.
2. The child may listen but be unable to articulate what his problem is, in which case the teacher would present the situation as she sees it with the different options available to the child to make friends and not to be taken in by the bully.
3. The child may be hostile and not listen at all, in which case the teacher would spell out her plan and tell the child that they will discuss the problem more fully when he is ready.

The options to the child are really the same in each example. In example 1, though, the child has the insight to make his own decisions once his options have been spelled out by the teacher. In example 2 the child wants to change but needs the support of the teacher. In example 3 the child is not ready to accept the problem; hence, he needs the structure overlayed on him by the teacher. In example 1 a psychodynamic approach is appropriate with the child internalizing the locus of control. Example 3 would require a learning theory approach with the locus of control being external (the teacher). Example 2 is somewhere in between.

But in each case the teacher would interpret the situation as she sees it and would show the child how to determine his options and how to implement them and accept the responsibility for them. In example 1 the teacher might ask the child what he might do to show his friendship to the other children in ways other than hitting them. She might further point out to the child how he is being used by the child that is setting him off. The teacher would also point out to the child his various options and their consequences in response to that child. His response-consequence options might be:

1. Ignore the other child and be praised by the teacher.
2. Hit the child and be punished himself.
3. Try to get along with the child and possibly make a friend.
4. Tell the child that he refuses to be upset and the other child might quit.

Although the choices are probably the same in each example, the differences involve the degree of student involvement in their development and the degree of teacher involvement in their implementation.

In either example the teacher verbally goes over how she and the child would arrive at their options. In time the teacher would expect the child to be able to recite and understand the steps. And through it all the teacher is stressing the need for compromise and flexibility. The child is offered opportunities to practice both either on his own or with close teacher supervision. Eventually the child will come to realize he does have options and that the power he has is not to allow others to push his button.

POTENTIAL PITFALLS

I am convinced that most teachers enter the teaching profession with the right intentions and noblest of ideals to help others learn and grow. I believe that they carry strong values, high goals, and enthusiasm to inspire others onward to better lives. Yet, too soon and to too many, something happens to these teachers that extinguishes most of their earlier enthusiasm and plans. However one might define the "system," I think teachers fall victim to the system, are generally unreinforced, ignored, unappreciated, and are confronted with a myriad of societal problems that they are expected to somehow deal with, when no one else seems to be able to deal with them. Teachers are under the gun to produce the seemingly impossible. After trying for two or three years many quit. The profession loses many good teachers this way. The ones that do stay need support and lots of it.

One of the more frequently discussed topics EC teachers talk about when they get together is teacher "burn-out." Working with EC students is so intense and emotionally demanding that one recent informal study by a colleague of mine showed the average classroom duration of EC teachers to be eighteen months! How does one stay "up" all the time while working with EC students, stay positive, and still retain one's sanity? This book has attempted to address this issue. I have attempted to describe in this chapter in particular the positive ways to enjoy teaching. We cannot afford to lose any more good teachers than is absolutely necessary. I am committed to the belief that the things I have discussed previously are essential to survival. In addition to those things already mentioned, teachers need to develop out-of-school interests, find some-one they can talk to, and leave the work at school when the day is done as much as is humanly possible.

Additionally, teachers should be aware of the most common pitfalls that contribute to frustration, dissatisfaction, and shortened teaching careers. If cognizant of frequently occurring problems, teachers can avoid them or deal with them quickly when they do occur. Emotional Conflict students need strong teachers, and the way to stay strong and adaptive is to live by the following rules.

DEVELOPING TEACHER STYLE

- Know yourself first
- Maintain objectivity
- Keep your options open
- Care enough to get involved
- Keep a strong sense of humor
- Get away from it all periodically
- Avoid pitfalls

Pitfalls

1. POWER STRUGGLES WITH STUDENTS. Teachers frequently get into situations with students in which the teacher feels compelled to win. Invariably when someone wins, someone else must lose. When we place ourselves and our students into win-lose situations, we destroy opportunities for trust development. Teachers of EC should be above having to win at the expense of students. We should seek opportunities where everyone involved can win. What we want are win-win situations (Gordon,1970). Win-win situations represent the achievement of a compromise. Compromise-reaching is a major portion of what an EC teacher's job is all about.

Teachers of EC do two things that place themselves into win-lose situations with their students. First, they frequently take the things EC kids say and do as a personal affront to them. They perceive that the child somehow has it in for them. The second thing that sets up confrontations and ultimately a win-lose situation is when the EC teacher asks the question "Why?"

Why did you do that? Why can you not behave? These are questions that are going to lead to problems. The kid has to lie, avoid the question, or ignore it altogether; this leads to entrapment. It's like the NIGYSOB game of TA (Berne, 1977). I set you up, knowing the answer to my question all along, then when you give me a different answer I reply with, "Ah-hah, now I've got you." Maybe so, but you've trapped the child, he is embarrassed and is not going to trust you.

Power struggles frequently develop between the class ring-leader and the teacher. Teachers subconsciously compete with this child to show him who has the biggest following or more "power." Power games serve no useful function and should be avoided. Too, teachers can force students into limited-response patterns. For instance, a child can make a derogatory remark in front of everyone; intended mostly to get a rise out of the teacher. Then the teacher, instead of ignoring the remarks, or waiting until the two are alone to correct, or whispering into the child's ear, chooses to make the child apologize or take a time-out. Either way, the child has limited responses and has lost pride and, consequently, does not care too much for his teacher.

2. UNREALISTIC GOAL SETTING. Teachers can guarantee student failure by setting unrealistic goals for them to achieve. Inexperienced teachers set their expectations too high (or sometimes too low) for their students, and when the child cannot live up to the expectations the child withdraws or becomes explosive. Teachers should periodically and automatically reassess their goals for their students to always insure success.

3. ENTERTAINING STUDENTS. Many teachers operate under the erroneous assumption that they must keep their students busy all the time while students are in their class. Part of this notion springs from the old teacher ethic that if your students are not busy and quiet, then you must not be a very good teacher. Students have come to expect the teacher to entertain them all the time. The result is students that do not know how to use their leisure time constructively. This is an area that the teacher should discuss with his/her students. They need to make decisions about the use of their leisure time and how to entertain themselves. This is a difficult area for teachers to relinquish. Busy hands are not necessarily happy hands if the busy is designed to occupy time and is not a meaningful exercise. The teacher should plan for unstructured time in each child's schedule so that he might plan its use for himself.

4. COMPETITION. Competition is a social malady, a condition that pervades the very fiber of American society. It is a contributory factor to children's emotional conflicts and, yet, confronts them in every effort to help them. Emotionally Conflicted children have long histories of failure. They have lost at most everything they have attempted. One of our goals is to give them success, to give them something that they are good at, even better than anyone else. This builds self-concept. Yet when we succeed at giving them this success, they stick it in the face of the other students and say, "See, I am better than you!" We tell students that the first one through wins the prize. Someone wins and someone loses. Hewett (1968) reports that competitive activities should not enter into classroom activities until the child is in the social level of learning competence. Yet most EC students are still functioning on the attention and response levels. There is probably no way to eliminate competition completely from the classroom, but every effort should be made to reduce its impact on the EC child until such time as he is ready to learn how to deal with it successfully so he will not get into trouble because of his inability to handle it.

5. PUNISHMENT AND TIME-OUT. To some teachers of the conflicted, punishment and time-out have come to be synonymous, when in actuality they are not. Punishment is the presentation of an aversive stimulus as a consequence of an unacceptable behavior. It tends to have immediate but limited effects and tends to suppress behaviors rather than extinguish them (Walker and Shea, 1976). *Time-out* is the removal of child from a reinforcing environment to a nonreinforcing one.

Punishment is generally the least effective of all the behavior modification techniques (Walker and Shea, 1976): however, if used conscientiously, sparingly, and under certain conditions punishment can be an effective tool (Redl, 1965). To send an EC child to the office for a paddling will have no effect on the child other than to become an unmeaningful event to be endured. Punishment is effective if administered by someone who has a relationship with a child. If a teacher and a child do have a meaningful relationship, and if the child so displeases the teacher that she feels a need to punish the child, then the message the child receives is that he has really upset his teacher, and if he wants to keep getting along with her then he better behave. Additionally, no punishment should be administered if the teacher is really angry. It is better for the teacher to simply say "I am so angry right now that if I punish you now, there is no telling what I might do. Instead, you sit here and think about what you have done and what you can do in the future to prevent this from happening again, while I cool down. I will be back then, and we can settle this at that time." Too, on repeated offenses, after the child has experienced your follow-through on carrying out promised punishments, it is not always necessary to carry out the actual act of punishment, if the child shows genuine remorse for his actions and can articulate what he might do to prevent future occurrences.

By definition, *time-out* means removal from a positive environment, not the administration of an aversive stimulus. In the context of the classroom, the classroom should be so reinforcing that the child cannot stand the thought of having to leave it. Therefore, he learns to restrain those behaviors that will get him sent out of the room or into time-out. However, most classrooms are not that reinforcing that time-out can be used as it is defined. Instead, time-out is frequently used as punishment, in that the child is presented with an aversive stimulus (the time-out-room), which has a short-term effect. Some children actually find the time-out room to be more reinforcing than the classroom. An effective compromise to this problem is to have a quiet corner in the room where children can sit to think about their actions or to cool off. I have frequently changed class activities when a child is sent to the quiet corner to engage the rest of the class in the most fun activity I can generate on the spot, in order to impress upon the timed-out child how much he is missing by being in time-out.

6. TEACHER RIGIDITY. When techniques have worked well for us in the past, we are reluctant to change and try new ones. Also, if we are in the middle

of a change program with a child and it is not working, we are reluctant to change suddenly and put the child on a new program. If something is not working, there is no known law that says we owe blind allegiance to that technique or program. It is perfectly acceptable to change to another course of action that might attain success for the child. The same flexibility that we want for our students we should also allow for ourselves.

Chapter 4

DEVELOPING AND MAINTAINING
A BALANCED PERSPECTIVE:
APPLICATION OF THE CONFLICT
RESOLUTION CURRICULUM

T O be effective at any job one must develop and maintain a balanced perspective about his/her overall goal(s). A proper sense of perspective helps one to keep a multitude of routine considerations and contradictions in balance. A more colloquial term would probably be the development of survival skills. This notion of perspective is likewise critical in working with emotional conflict (EC) children. Piaget meticulously detailed our biologically rooted and natural need to achieve equilibrium in our world by developing an understanding or sense of order out of the chaos that surrounds us. Most practitioners in the profession of providing services to EC children would certainly agree that there is a great deal of chaos in the everyday world of working with EC children. But how do we achieve equilibrium? All influences considered, it has become critical that teachers and therapists be able to maintain a healthy perspective towards their goals in order to be effective. However, in the field of emotional conflict there have been continued influences that have made it difficult to survive. Teacher burnout is one direct, observable fallout of this imbalance in the field. In the EC field, as is true in many fields today, there exists a dichotomy between theory and application. Both are necessary, but we are not always successful at bringing the two together. This dichotomy has hindered our individual efforts to create order in a field that suffers from chronic disarray. Theorists attempt to answer the "why" of misbehavior and practitioners address the "what" to do about misbehavior. To further complicate the whys and whats, it seems that we have many kinds of whys (i.e. learning theory vs. psychodynamic theory, etc.) and many kinds of whats (i.e. structure vs. nonstructure, etc.). What we have long needed is a compromise of reason. We exist in a world perceived by many to be black and white, when in reality most social issues are shadowed grey. The Conflict Resolution Curriculum (CRC) represents a realistic compromise. The CRC stresses a balanced perspective for the practioner; a perspective founded in both theory and day-to-day practicality.

Chapter 1 discussed the state of the art in EC. Such a review can help clarify one's sense of perspective in that we should consider as many of the issues as possible and then make some decisions concerning our opinions about those issues. One of the more subtle deficits discernable from such a review was the absence of a generally comprehensive curriculum oriented to providing theoretically based goals, objectives, activities, and evaluations for writing IEP's for the EC child. The result of this need was the Conflict Resolution Curriculum (See Chap.2). Chapter 3 detailed specific ideas on how to make the CRC work. The CRC is simply a guide for dealing with the why and what of the EC child. Chapter 3 also dealt with the critical ingredient for experiencing success with the EC child, i.e. the teacher-therapist's personality.

What I wanted to share in this final chapter, beyond my concern for a balanced perspective, was some of the techniques and influences that have traditionally worked well for teachers working with EC children. There are undoubtedly hundreds of influences that collectively shape the development of a successful teacher-therapist. True, too, is the fact that in attempting to communicate these influences to others something is invariably lost in the translation. The loss is due substantially to the semantic shortcomings of the different connotations attached to frequently used words that describe our field. In the last chapter I tried to enunciate some of the influences that tend to mold good teachers, but I know that some of the strength or degree of importance placed upon them by me will unfortunately be lost in their reading. Consequently, at this point I want to again, albeit in different words, attempt to capture the essence of what I sought to communicate to the reader in the last chapter about the criticalness of certain concepts necessary to the development and maintenance of a balanced perspective.

Influences that are worth mentioning can be arranged into two groups. The first group includes those ideas of unknown origin but belonging to the public domain. They may be commonly known by all, but tend not to be identifiable with any single person, while the second group contains ideas generally attributed as originating with a specific person or persons. Members of the first group would include the value of experience, trusting in yourself, anticipation, the style of your approach, and the value of good listening.

Experience can be the best teacher of all if we simply allow ourselves to be receptive to our varied experiences. We can learn from both good and bad experiences, but unfortunately many of us do not take advantage of the learning opportunities afforded us by our experiences. Confidence in our ability to serve children is directly proportional to the experiences that we bring to each uniquely different situation. Trust in our abilities is partially founded upon these experiences. With so many different opinions available for the asking on how to work with problem children it becomes difficult to decide who to believe, therefore each of us must learn to trust ourselves. Assuming careful deliberation over issues, opinions, and techniques, and assuming a decision has been made regarding individual style, then why not trust in yourself to do what is ultimately best for the child? Part of trusting in your own abilities is not always waiting for someone else to tell you what to do, but rather having enough confidence in your own talents to intervene appropriately. I continue to find a significant number of teachers that have good ideas, but do not trust themselves enough to follow through on them.

Anticipation as a concept represents all of the things a teacher might do to prevent problems with EC children before they occur. If we know enough about our children and can learn to predict what they might do before they do the deed, then the child is much easier to redirect or correct. Anticipation also means looking at your EC children from their perspective to learn how they think and how they are motivated. Anticipation can lead to increased understanding and heightened awareness of how the EC child perceives his world, since frequently the EC child does not see the world the same as you or I.

Style of approach was discussed in greater detail previously, but to recap, style deals with the manner in which the teacher has elected to approach her students, i.e. authoritarian, autocratic, open, closed, etc. The basic tenet of style is to approach each problem situation with a matter-of-fact air that conveys to the child that at least one of you is in control of his emotions. This approach reduces the likelihood that everyone is going to become angry in a crisis. This anger diminishes the likelihood for any potential growth resultant from the crisis.

The final member of the first group deals with developing good listening skills. Many of us listen well but do not hear what is being said. Good listening requires our full attention and genuine effort to understand what is being said. There are several authors that have suggested methods for developing good listening habits, and they are recommended highly for further reading (Dinkmeyer and McKay, 1976; Gordon, 1970, Rogers, 1954).

The second group contains the ideas offered by recognized leaders in the field. These ideas have become for me the prevailing influences that have shaped my sense of perspective for working with EC children. I place no particular value of one idea over another, for as I have said these represent a collective group that have been utilized over the years. Specifically I have found the work of the following people most beneficial: Carl Rogers, William Glasser, Frank Hewett, Judy Margolis and Barbara Keogh, Lew Linkous, Hill Walker and Henry Reinert. Rogers has been a significant influence for at least three identifiable reasons and most assuredly others that are not so easily listed. Rogers (1958) was one of the first to deal with counselor empathy, congruence, and self-selection of goals. Counselor empathy deals with the techniques employed by the counselor to tune-in to the emotional level of the client. Further, Rogers described how the counselor should encourage the client to work through his/her particular problem without the counselor really interjecting himself into the client's line of reasoning. This was accomplished by showing genuine regard for the client and by not asking questions, lecturing, probing, interjecting personal values, etc. Rogers's work in this area obviously influenced the development of Gordon's (1970) active listening concepts and Dinkmeyer's (1976) reflective listening. Rogers's concept of congruence be-

tween one's real and ideal self has helped me to realize how I perceive myself
and how others perceive me may not always be similar or congruent. Consequently I must make a conscientious effort to ensure that how I think I am coming across with children is in fact how they perceive me. Too frequently
teachers perceive themselves as being open and receptive, while the children
they are teaching perceive them as rigid and closed. As an example, we all have
probably encountered the person attracted to working with children in conflict
because of the perceived opportunity to do their own thing, to "free-wheel" it,
and to be open and unstructured, only to find themselves frustrated by their in-
effectiveness. These same people are likewise perceived by their students as
unstructured and unorganized. The third influence of Rogers has been in self-
selection of goals. When I first started working with EC children, I thought that
I had to determine where they were emotionally, and then determine by myself
the direction of their therapy and hence their goals for emotional development.
What I was omitting was the child himself. By assuming that the child thought
as I did, and had the same middle class values I had, I was disallowing the setting from which the child came and in which he would be going back into, as
well as his own needs. Reading Rogers helped me to realize that since I could
not *make* a child learn or even *make* him behave that I really ought to include
him in the goal-setting portion of his intervention plan. This would at least help
insure his investment in the intervention plan, because he would be working
towards a goal mutually selected rather than one I had selected.

William Glasser's influence is very simple and short, but so important that I
think of it every day. Early in his book, *Reality Therapy* (1975), he stated two
universal needs of *all* people: the need to love and to be loved, and the need to
feel worthwhile. Translating these two statements into practice I always attempt to show my love for EC children by demonstrating a genuine acceptance
of each child. I show him that while his behavior is not always acceptable, he is.
Then I teach him how to express his emotions. His sense of being worthwhile is
developed by pointing out his positive traits, encouraging his independence,
noting his contributions, and by allowing him to make decisions that are
followed through on by all.

Frank Hewett's contribution has been his developmental sequences of
educational goals (1968) or levels of learning competence (1980). Too frequently teachers start their intervention on a level that is too difficult for the child.
Yet how is anyone to know where to start and where to proceed? Hewett (1980)
provides a realistic answer in his goals, i.e. attention, response, order, ex-
ploratory, social mastery, and achievement (achievement is not included in his
second edition work). These levels of competence are hierarchial in that
mastery at one level is required to move onto the next. To be emphasized is
that we typically ask EC students to develop "order" in their environments
when in actuality they are still not even attending, or we introduce competitive
situations that require higher levels of competence than the child may be able

to handle at the time.

Barbara Keogh and Judy Margolis at UCLA have initiated several investigations (1974, 1975) into attentional and compensatory characteristics of children with educational deficits. Some of their conclusions have been predictable, while others have been startling. Predictable were their conclusions that children definitely develop compensatory mechanisms to solve problems where they are unable to solve them by traditional avenues. Startling were their results that implied that a majority of learning problems were in fact attentional problems. Basically the child was not attending properly. They define "attention" as a construct and not a unitary event. As a construct attention is comprised of four functions: (1) a physiological state in which the child is alerted or aroused to an event; (2) focusing and selective attention; (3) distractibility to outside events; and (4) sustaining that attention. Ross (1976) says much the same thing. The application for EC children is to ascertain their "attending" skills and then improve upon them.

Lou Linkous has provided the theoretical base from which I operate. In his *Transactional Systems Approach* to behavior is provided a thoughtful and methodical system to comfortably handle the totality of the six various models used to explain emotional conflict (see Chap. 1). The resolution Linkous's systems approach provides to the problem of which of the six models to use increases one's effectiveness with the emotional conflict child, because it allows the user to use a consolidation of the six models, e.g. biophysical, sociological, behavioral, ecological, psychodynamic, and counter-theory (Rhodes and Tracy, 1972).

Hill Walker's *Problem Behavior Identification Checklist* (1976) is the most useful checklist commercially available. Although a screening instrument, the tool yields many different kinds of information. Additionally, the checklist lends itself to a natural flow into the behavior types discussed by Reinert (1976).

The Walker has the following advantages:

1. The instrument is simple to use, which aids in getting it filled out by teachers.
2. The instrument is quick to administer.
3. The Walker describes behaviors most typically associated with EC children. Many times a teacher will ask to fill out a Walker on a problem child, only to hand it back and say that these statements do not apply to her "problem" child, but she does have one that they do fit. Thus the Walker is an educational tool to educate those that are unfamiliar with true EC children.
4. The Walker allows for multiple comparisons. Always try to get at least three teachers to answer the questions about the same child. If their responses are similar then the child can be seen as consistent and probably experiencing a problem. Yet, if the child is viewed differently by all the teachers, then the teachers can be said to have the problem. This tells

the EC teacher where to initiate intervention — with the EC child or with the individual teacher.

5. Walker, like Reinert, has been successful in most accurately describing the behaviors most commonly encountered by teachers. Many psychiatric terms (DSM-III, 1980) simply are not usable to the everyday EC teacher. Walker's terminology leads directly into Reinert's groups of behavior, thus providing some consistency from screening to intervention.

6. The *Profile Analysis Chart* (PAC) provides a graphic method to determine priorities in getting services to children. Walker identifies a T-score of 60 as being the cut-off point. Any individual scale score falling above this cut-off point is an indication for further study or diagnosis. The most common pattern seen in my experience has been a "W" pattern (see Chart). This pattern matches Reinert's acting-out child and in reality is the easiest child to work with, because he is giving the teacher many modifiable behaviors. However, when the child's scores are higher in withdrawal or disturbed peer relations, the EC teacher should become most concerned and seriously start to question whether or not this child indeed has a personality problem.

7. As the first part of a three-tool battery, the Walker provides useful information for planning intervention strategies. The second tool is an observation form compiled by EC teachers based primarily on the Walker, that gives a guide for classroom observations of the potential EC child (*see* Appendix A). The third tool is the *Piers-Harris Children's Self-Concept Scale* (1969) by Ellen V. Piers and Dale Harris (*see* Appendix B). The Piers-Harris provides useful information about how the child feels about himself and is given when the EC teacher first interviews the child. Subsequently, upon comparison all three instruments begin to yield a realistic profile of the child.

Finally I come to Henry Reinert's four basic behavioral patterns (1976). Many attempts have been made to group, characterize, and label deviant behavior (*see* Hewett, 1980, pp.36-40; Kauffman, 1977, pp. 27-30; Kirk, 1972, pp. 390-392). Most of the classifications appeared to be clinically oriented. Frequently the clinically derived terminology was of little value to the classroom teacher because the terms were foreign or did not practically fit the types of behaviors the teacher was seeing. As Reinert himself points out (1976, p. 131), no single child ever meshes completely into one category. Reinert's categories do the best job of describing the types of behaviors most commonly encountered by teachers of emotional conflict children. Reinert's (1976) four types with a short description of each are listed below.

1. ACTING-OUT BEHAVIORS. This is the most frequently encountered group of behaviors, due in part to their high visibility in the classroom. Although this is the most frequently referred group, it is also the easiest type of behavior to

Walker Problem Behavior Identification Checklist

Revised 1976
by Hill M. Walker, Ph.D.

Published by

WESTERN PSYCHOLOGICAL SERVICES
PUBLISHERS AND DISTRIBUTORS
12031 WILSHIRE BOULEVARD
LOS ANGELES, CALIFORNIA 90025

A DIVISION OF MANSON WESTERN CORPORATION

Name:	School:
Address:	Grade:
Age: Sex: M F Date:	Classroom:
Rated By: Position of Rater:	

INSTRUCTIONS

Please read each statement carefully and respond by circling the number to the right of the statement if you have observed that behavioral item in the child's response pattern during the last two month period. If you have not observed the behavior described in the statement during this period, do not circle any numbers (in other words, make no marks whatsoever if the statement describes behavior which is NOT present).

Examples:

Scales

	1	2	3	4	5

1. Has temper tantrums .... ②
2. Has no friends 4
3. Refers to himself as dumb, stupid, or incapable 3
4. Must have approval for tasks attempted or completed. .... ①

Statements 1 and 4 are considered to be present while statements 2 and 3 are considered to be absent. Therefore, only the numbers to the right of items 1 and 4 are circled, and the numbers to the right of 2 and 3 are NOT circled.

Profile Analysis Chart (PAC)

Characteristic "W" Pattern

Cut-off

W-97A

change, because the child is giving many behaviors that are modifiable; that is, he is at least doing something. This group is generally considered as not having personality problems, but rather as having learned the wrong set of rules by which to operate. Descriptors of this group would be asocial, aggressive, and defiant. This type of child can most easily be worked with in his natural environment (not the EC class) by implementing an appropriate behavior modification program.

2. WITHDRAWING BEHAVIORS. The overly quiet child has historically been viewed as not in need of EC service. They are quiet and present no problems at all. They are usually labeled as shy and are left alone. In recent years this child has been recognized as really needing help, and attempts have been made more and more to do so. The withdrawn child is experiencing some personality problems. Anxiety is a key descriptor of this child. Whether the perception is warranted or not, this child is unable to cope with the pressure they are feeling to achieve or perform at some high level. Their choice is to opt-out or withdraw. This child requires careful consideration and help in selecting and accepting reasonable standards and goals. Possible sources of outside pressure should be considered and dealt with to help the child gain insight into handling the anxiety they have bottled-up inside.

3. DEFENSIVE BEHAVIORS. These behaviors usually describe various mild personality problems and require longer and more sensitive intervention to correct than do acting-out behaviors. Anxiety is again a key descriptor but is manifested in acts of avoidance. The child does not want any attention brought to the fact that they are somehow inadequate. The child is typically the class clown, or the child whose dog ate his homework, etc. This child is a manipulator, cries, lies, and/or daydreams frequently. Acceptance of responsibility is a major goal of intervention focusing on the development of an internal locus of control. This child would probably be labeled as having mild neurosis if a psychiatric classification system were used.

4. DISORGANIZED BEHAVIORS. This child has only recently appeared in the public schools (via PL 94-142). Historically, the disorganized child has been perceived as suffering from a psychosis and has been institutionalized. The prognosis for recovery to a level of self-sufficiency is around one child in twelve. The disorganized child requires intensive one-on-one and generally expensive long-term services. Autistic and schizophrenic children would be included in this group.

The above-mentioned influences can provide a systematic procedure for working with EC children. As such they have served as the basis for my teacher training programs. There is consistency among the various influences, and they are based on considerations of importance to the day-to-day intervention with emotional conflict children, i.e. they are rooted in practicality. What I want to do now is to illustrate in synoptic form some of the various points mentioned in the book. I have selected four "typical" cases. I will describe their behaviors, how they were identified, and how they were planned for using the CRC.

CASE STUDIES

Child Number One

Child number one was a ten-year-old boy in the fourth grade. His present-

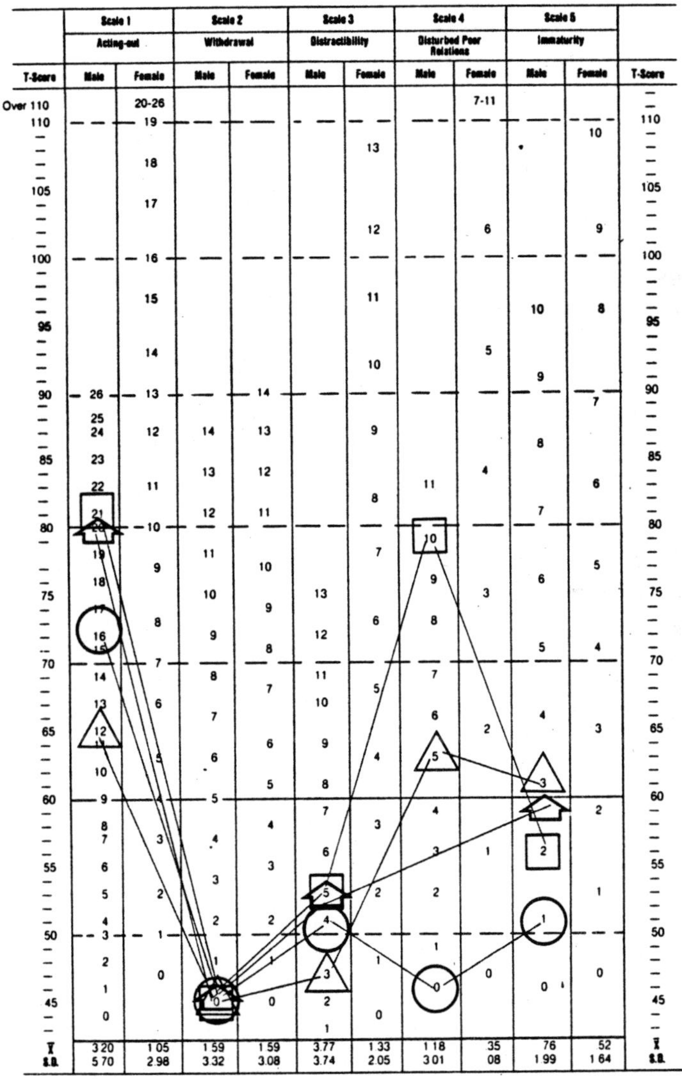

Figure 4-1. Child Number One's Walker. Copyright 1970, 1976 by Hill M. Walker, Ph.D. All rights reserved. Reprinted by permission of Hill M. Walker, Ph.D.

ing behaviors were aggression, crying, abusive language, fire-setting, and extreme frustration. After obtaining parental consent for testing, Walker Behavior Checklists were given to four teachers to complete on the child. Their responses are shown in Figure 4-1. Careful examination of this child's profile will show reasonably similar perceptions about the child by all four raters. The child is seen as exhibiting significant acting-out behaviors and some disturbed peer relations. By examining the actual responses of the raters on the back of the form a collection of descriptors was compiled. The collection of more descriptors continued with psychological and academic testing, observations, and interviews with the child.

There are certainly many tests available for use in obtaining a psychological profile of a child. Many psychometrists use the WISC-R, the Bender Visual-Motor Gestalt test, and the House-Tree-Person test as the core of their evaluation. While their validity and results may be questionable for diagnosing EC children, administrative constraints still require their use. The most reliable information will be secured from observations and interviews. Hence, by studying the Walker profiles, by making at least two observations on this child using the Emotional Conflict Observation Form (*See* Appendix A) (or any suitable observation form), and after having talked with him one-on-one on two occasions, we then had a large collection of information, all of which confirmed the presenting behaviors.

After a meeting with the appropriate school personnel and the child's mother the following goals for intervention were reached:

1. The child needs to exercise control over his constant attention-seeking behaviors.
2. The child needs to confront his problems, rather than storm off.
3. The child needs opportunities to develop more confidence in himself.
4. The child needs to express his feelings more appropriately.
5. The child should be encouraged to develop his innate leadership abilities.

Turning next to our curriculum guide, the group identified six problem areas in which the child was manifesting problems.

Problem Area

1B Student engages in actions not directed toward others but intended to disrupt or actually results in classroom disruption.
1C Student engages in actions physically directed toward others/environment.
2A Inappropriate perceptions of one's feelings.
2D Inappropriate perceptions of one's social responsibility.
2E Inappropriate perceptions of others and the environment.
3C Student does not respond appropriately to outside communication.

From these six problem areas the group had twenty-five objectives from which to choose. Twenty-five were too many for the child to start with, so only six of the more critical objectives were selected; the objectives are listed below. Their corresponding activities and evaluations can be found by examining the CRC in Chapter 2.

1B (Objective #2). Student will verbalize and implement alternatives to his usual inappropriate attention-seeking behaviors.

1C (Objective #2). Student demonstrates respect for physical and psychological space of others.

2A (Objective #3). Student can accurately describe his present emotional state.

2D (Objective #2). Student demonstrates his ability to assume responsibility for himself and his actions.

2E (Objective #1). Student can cope with other's feelings toward him.

3C (Objective #1). Student will accurately express thoughts and feelings in words to others.

By transferring these objectives to the child's IEP, his program of intervention was ready to implement. Note that all three goals listed in the CRC are being addressed. The curriculum has built-in redundancy or a back-up system to mutually support each of the objectives. This is accomplished by the fact that the various objectives frequently tend to address the same type of problems but with a different perspective, reflected in the actual wording of each objective. The outcome with this child was great success. In less than a year's time he was fully integrated back into regular classes with no need for follow-up support. This entire process of checklists, observations, interviews, testing, group consensus of goal selections, identification of problem areas, objectives selection, and implementation may appear overwhelming, initially. True it is a slow process to the inexperienced, but with experience and practice the process speeds up until you reach a point where all the paperwork is gathered, not to tell you what to do but to legitimize or document your already formed opinions. Learn to trust in your own abilities to draw succinct and accurate conclusions about programming for EC children.

Child Number Two

Child number two was a fifteen-year-old female in the tenth grade with defensive/disorganized behaviors. Her grades were D's and F's when she even attended school. Her presenting behaviors were denial of wrongdoing or responsibility for personal actions, argumentative, self-isolating in groups, engagement in homosexual behavior, temper tantrums, attempted suffocation of a sibling, and abusive language, all manifested in aperiodic episodes.

The remarkable agreement by the raters on the Walker underscored the consistency of this child's maladaptive behaviors as perceived by those around her (*See* Fig. 4-2). Observations and interviews confirmed her extreme dislike for herself and her unwillingness to try to get along with others. At this child's planning meeting the general consensus for goals were stated as follows:

1. She needs to more adequately express her feelings and problems when feeling excessive stress.
2. She needs to check herself before she allows herself to become so destructive to her environment.
3. She needs counseling to address her homosexuality.
4. She needs practice in approaching and communicating with adults.
5. She needs to learn skills for group participation.

	Scale 1 Acting-out		Scale 2 Withdrawal		Scale 3 Distractibility		Scale 4 Disturbed Peer Relations		Scale 5 Immaturity		
T-Score	Male	Female	Male	Female	Male	Female	Male	Female	Male	Female	T-Score
X̄ S.D.	3.20 5.70	1.05 2.98	1.59 3.32	1.59 3.08	3.77 3.74	1.33 2.05	1.18 3.01	.35 .08	.76 1.99	.52 1.64	X̄ S.D.

Figure 4-2. Child Number Two's Walker. Copyright 1970, 1976 by Hill M. Walker, Ph.D. All rights reserved. Reprinted by permission of Hill M. Walker, Ph.D.

These goals were then matched with the CRC problem areas, and certain corresponding objectives were selected.

Problem Area

1B Student engages in actions not directed toward others but intended to disrupt or actually results in classroom disruptions.

1C Student engages in actions physically directed toward others/environment.

2A Inappropriate perceptions of one's feelings.

2B Inappropriate perceptions of one's body.

2C Inappropriate perception of one's coping skills.

3C Student does not respond appropriately to outside communication.

1B (Objective #2). Student will verbalize and implement alternatives to her usual inappropriate attention-seeking behaviors.

1C (Objective #5). Student will engage in appropriate sex role behavior.

2A (Objective #1). Student will successfully differentiate between constructive and destructive emotions.

2A (Objective #3). Student can accurately describe her present emotional state.

2B (Objective #1). Student demonstrates a positive awareness of her body.

2B (Objective #3). Student is able to explain the relationship of her body and sexuality.

2C (Objective #2). Student can articulate effect of emotions on one's coping skills.

3C (Objective #1). Student will accurately express thoughts and feelings in words to others.

Outcome

This girl sought out and found attachment to female adults. Typically this arrangement was able to maintain the girl in adaptive behavior. The fact that her episodes were infrequent or aperiodic allowed plenty of counseling opportunities. The child was likable and very helpful. In time she was able to control her emotional and destructive outbursts. She was seen by others as performing well, but her thinking processes continued to effect her ability to "fit in." She still isolates herself, still defies adult authority more than is socially acceptable, and continues in bisexual behaviors.

Child Number Three

Child number three was a third-grade male exhibiting defensive/acting-out behaviors. His presenting behaviors were excessive temper tantrums, destructiveness, sociopathic, manipulative, incapable of crying or showing any range of emotion, lying, and stealing.

The Walker showed agreement in the type of pattern, but does differ in the degree (*See* Fig.4-3). The degree was effected by the difference in exposure to this child's manipulative and sociopathic behaviors. Again, after all the data collection was complete and the group meeting held to decide placement and services, the following goals were established:

1. The child should learn to accept limits from adults.

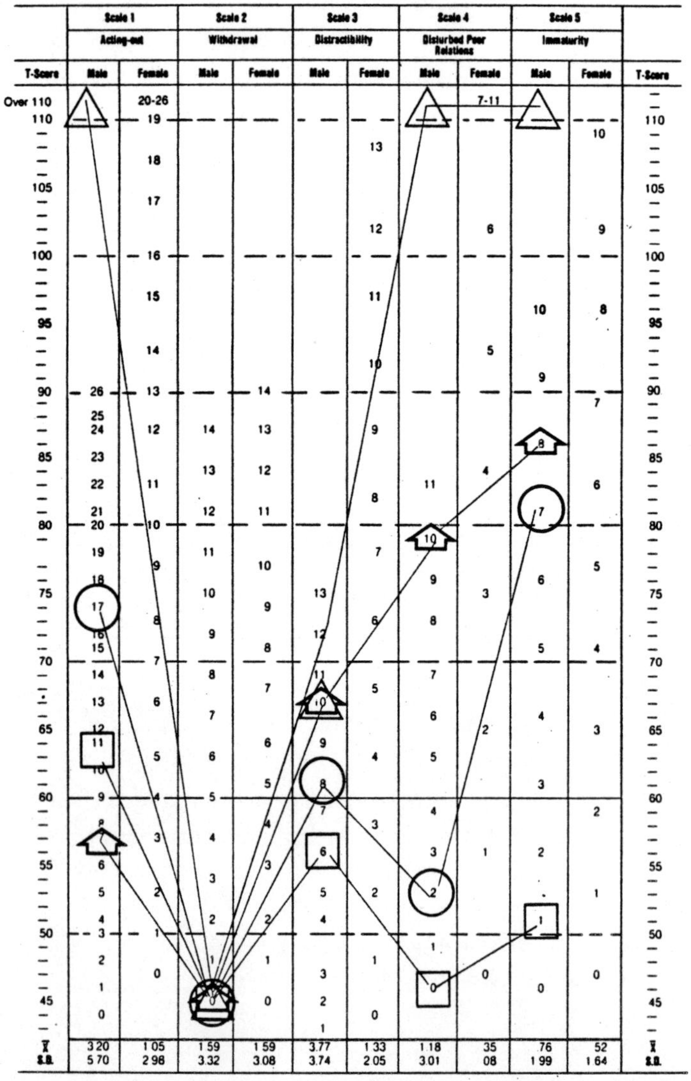

Figure 4-3. Child Number Three's Walker. Copyright 1970, 1976 by Hill M. Walker, Ph.D. All rights reserved. Reprinted by permission of Hill M. Walker, Ph.D.

2. The child needs to learn to display genuine feelings for self and others.
3. The child needs to eliminate lying and stealing behavior.
4. Child needs to accept responsibility for his own behavior.
5. Child needs to develop group play skills.

CRC problem areas and objectives from these goals are listed below:

Problem Area

1B Student engages in actions not directed toward others but intended to disrupt or actually results in classroom disruptions.
1C Student engages in actions physically directed toward others/environment.
2A Inappropriate perceptions of one's feelings.
2D Inappropriate perceptions of one's social responsibilities.
2E Inappropriate perceptions of others and the environment.
3A Student is not receiving communication from the environment.
3B Student is not comprehending communication attempts.

1B (Objective #2). Student will verbalize and implement alternatives to his usual inappropriate attention-seeking behaviors.
1B (Objective #3). Student participates appropriately with others in a group setting.
1C (Objective #2). Student demonstrates respect for physical and psychological space of others.
2A (Objective #3). Student can accurately describe his present emotional state.
2D (Objective #2). Student is able to assume his responsibility to larger society by practicing adaptive conformity.
2E (Objective #2). Student learns how to deal with rejection and non-trustable individuals.
3A (Objective #2). Student recognizes and successfully interprets nonverbal message from others.
3B (Objective #1). Student verbally or physically acknowledges receipt of outside communication.
3B (Objective #2). Student comprehends that others in his world have needs and is able to correctly identify them.
3C (Objective #3). Student accepts the need for and engages in consensus reaching (compromise) in communication.

Outcome

This type of child is extremely difficult to work with. If success comes, it comes begrudgingly and slow. After a year, this child was just starting to ex-

90 *Conflict Resolution Curriculum*

press emotion and to be aware of his manipulative techniques. Then he moved, and no word has been heard from him, his parents, or schools, so final outcome is unknown.

Child Number Four

Child number four was a junior-high-aged female with severe defensive/disorganized behaviors (*See* Fig. 4-4). Presenting behaviors were schizophrenia, enuresis, encopresis, withdrawal, disoriented thought processes,

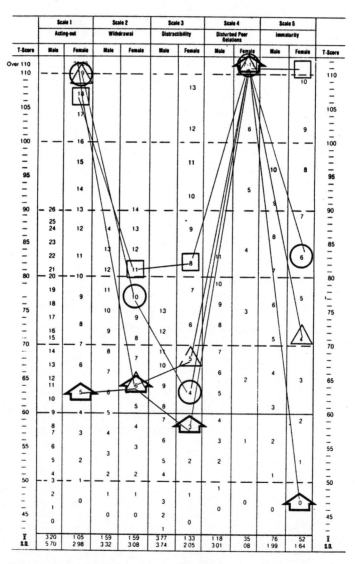

Figure 4-4. Child Number Four's Walker. Copyright 1970, 1976 by Hill M. Walker, Ph.D. All rights reserved. Reprinted by permission of Hill M. Walker, Ph.D.

and destructiveness. Her goals were determined as follows:

1. Child should eliminate encopretic and enuretic behaviors.
2. Child needs increased group participation.
3. Child needs to learn how to ventilate her anger and frustration appropriately.
4. Child needs to develop a positive image of herself.

CRC problem areas and objectives based upon above state goals were selected.

Problem area

1D Student engages in inappropriate activities that are biologically rooted or manifested.
2A Inappropriate perceptions of one's feelings.
2B Inappropriate perceptions of one's body.
2C Inappropriate perceptions of one's coping skills.
2E Inappropriate perceptions of others and the environment.
3A Student is not receiving communication from the environment.
3C Student does not respond appropriately to outside communication.

1D (Objective #2). Student will demonstrate improved self-care skills.
2A (Objective #3). Student can accurately describe her present emotional state.
2B (Objective #1). Student demonstrates a positive awareness of her body.
2B (Objective #4). Student develops the values necessary for caring for her body.
2C (Objective #2). Student can articulate effect of emotions on one's coping skills.
2E (Objective #3). Student demonstrates ability to discriminately trust others and environment.
3A (Objective #2). Student can initiate and sustain appropriate listening skills.
3C (Objective #1). Student verbally or physically acknowledges receipt of outside communication.
3C (Objective #3). Student accepts the need for and engages in consensus reaching (compromise) in communication.

Outcome

The interesting aspect of this child was that substantial progress was made during a year of intervention. This child was maintained or supported successfully in the EC program. After a year of self-contained EC classes, she was mainstreamed with acceptable success. The second year she was placed in a new foster home. This type of movement appears to be very common with EC children: hence, compounding any sustained intervention. This girl eventually experienced an acute episode that marked a turning away from progress. She has been reinstitutionalized.

APPENDICES

EMOTIONAL CONFLICT OBSERVATION FORM

CHILD'S NAME _____ DATE OF BIRTH _____

SCHOOL _____ DATE OF OBSERVATION _____

NAME OF OBSERVER_____ POSITION _____

OBSERVATION NO.____

ACTIVITY	TIME OF DAY	CHARACTERISTIC OBSERVED	LENGTH OF OBSERVATION

		1. Self-Image_____
		
		 2. Social Interaction _____
		
		 3. Teacher Relationship(s) _____
		
		 4. Classroom Activities_____
		
		 5. Peer Relationship_____
		 Socialized
		 Unsocialized
		 Other
		 6. Personality Reflections
		    a. Hypersensitive
		
		    b. Inferiority Feelings
		
		    c. Acting Out
		
		    d. Withdrawn
		
		    e. Distractibility
		
		    f. Immaturity
		
		    g. Other	

OBSERVATION BEHAVIOR CHECKLIST
(Check those statements depicting observed behavior.)

Acting-Out Behaviors

☐ 1. Child appears to engage in excessive amount of verbal abuse (cursing, arguing, defiance, lying).
☐ 2. Child's physical actions tend to be excessive (self-mutilation, destroying property, throwing objects).
☐ 3. Child is quick-tempered.
☐ 4. Child overcompensates or rationalizes.
☐ 5. Child wants to be the center of attention.

Withdrawn Behaviors

☐ 1. Child is not open to new experiences.
☐ 2. Child shows little or no emotions — "flat effect."
☐ 3. Child does not speak up in class discussion.
☐ 4. Child generally plays alone.
☐ 5. Child appears to feel unhappy.

Distractibility

☐ 1. Child does not keep his mind on planned activity.
☐ 2. Child is unable to attend to and complete new tasks.
☐ 3. Child is not a good listener.
☐ 4. Child does not follow instructions easily and quickly.
☐ 5. Child appears to have a very short attention span.

Disturbed Peer Relations

☐ 1. Child does not seem to be popular.
☐ 2. Child does not seem to want to make new friends.
☐ 3. Child does not seem to want to feel important to his/her friends.
☐ 4. Child does not act friendly toward others.
☐ 5. Child does not get along with people his/her own age.

Immaturity

☐ 1. Child will not "own up" if he makes a mistake.
☐ 2. Student prefers to play with younger students.
☐ 3. Child provokes or manipulates peers/others.
☐ 4. Child avoids responsibility.
☐ 5. Child always says "I can't do it," is whiny, and/or cries without provocation.

THE PIERS-HARRIS CHILDREN'S SELF CONCEPT SCALE

(The Way I Feel About Myself)

Here are a set of statements. Some of them are true of you and so you will circle the *yes*. Some are not true of you and so you will circle the *no*. Answer *every* question even if some are hard to decide, but do *not* circle both *yes* and *no*. Remember, circle the *yes* if the statement is generally like you, or circle the *no* if the statement is generally not like you. There are no right or wrong answers. Only you can tell us how you feel about yourself, so we hope you will mark the way you really feel inside.

1. My classmates make fun of me ....yes   no
2. I am a happy person ....yes   no
3. It is hard for me to make friends...yes   no
4. I am often sad...yes   no
5. I am smart...yes   no
6. I am shy ....yes   no

This Scale was developed by Ellen V. Piers, Ph.D. and Dale B. Harris, Ph.D. and was reprinted in part by permission of Counselor Recordings and Tests, Box 6184 Acklen Station, Nashville, Tennessee 37212.

REFERENCES

Argyris, C., and Schon, D.A.: *Theory in Practice: Increasing Professional Effectiveness.* San Francisco, Jossey-Bass, 1974.

Bender, M., and Valletutti, P.J.: *Teaching the Moderately and Severely Handicapped: Curriculum Objectives, Strategies and Activities.* Baltimore, University Park Press, 1976.

Berne, E.: *Games People Play.* New York, Grove Press, 1964.

Bower, E.M.: *Early Identification of Emotionally Handicapped Children in School,* 2nd Ed. Springfield, Thomas, 1969.

Cratty, B.: *Active Learning: Games to Enhance Academic Abilities.* Englewood Cliffs, Prentice-Hall, 1971.

Delacato, C. H. : *Neurological Organization and Reading.* Springfield, Thomas, 1966.

Dinkmeyer, D., and McKay, G.D.: *Parent's Handbook, Systematic Training for Effective Parenting.* Circle Pines, Minnesota, American Guidance Service, 1976.

Dyer, W.W.: *Your Erroneous Zones.* New York, Avon, 1977.

— — —: *Pulling Your Own Strings.* New York, Avon, 1979.

Erikson, E.: *Childhood and Society,* 2nd Ed. New York, Norton, 1963.

Glasser, W.: *Reality Therapy.* New York, Harper and Row, 1965.

Gordon, T.: *P.E.T.: Parent Effectiveness Training.* New York, Wyden, 1970.

Haring, N.G. (Ed.): *Behavior of Exceptional Children,* 2nd Ed. Columbus, Merrill, 1978.

Hewett, F.M., and Taylor, F.D.: *The Emotionally Disturbed Child in the Classroom: The Orchestration of Success,* 2nd Ed. Boston, Allyn and Bacon, 1980.

Kauffman, J.M.: *Characteristics of Children's Behavior Disorders.* Columbus, Merrill, 1977.

Kirk, S.A.: *Educating Exceptional Children.* Boston, Houghton-Mifflin, 1972.

Lewis-Smith, J.: *Non-verbal Communication in the Classroom: Report Analysis and Critique of Evaluative Instruments.* ERIC-ED-145-490, June, 1977.

McDonald, P., and McDonald, D.: *Guilt-Free.* New York, Grosset and Dunlap, 1977.

Margolis, J.S., and Keogh, B.K.: School Achievement and Ability to Maintain Attention to Task: A Vigilance Model Applied to School Learning. Paper presented at the Annual Meeting of the Western Psychological Association, San Francisco, 1974.

— — —: Attentional Characteristics of Children with Educational Problems: A Functional Analysis. Technical Report SERP 1975-A7, UCLA, 1975.

Mehrabian, A.: *Non-verbal Communication.* Chicago, Aldine, 1972.

Newcomb, T., in Tauris, C.: What does college do for a person? Frankly very little. *Psychology Today, 1974.*

Piers, E.V., and Harris, D.B.: *Piers-Harris Children's Self Concept Scale.* Nashville, Counselor Recordings and Tests, 1969.

Rankin, D.: *What Teachers Say May Not Be What Students Hear: Non-verbal Communication in the Classroom.* ERIC-ED-150-142, January, 1978.

Redl, F.: The concept of punishment. In Long, Morse, and Newman (Eds.): *Conflict in the Classroom.* Belmont, California, Wadsworth, 1965.

Reinert, H.R.: *Children in Conflict.* St. Louis, Mosby, 1976.

Rhodes, W.C., and Tracy, M.L.: *A Study of Child Variance: Conceptual Models.* Ann Arbor, University of Michigan Press, 1972, volume 1.

Rogers, C.R.: A process conception of psychotherapy. *American Psychologist, 13:*142-149, 1958.

Ross, A.O.: *Psychological Aspects of Learning Disabilities and Reading Disorders*. New York, McGraw Hill, 1976.

Rothman, E.: *The Angel Inside Went Sour*. New York, D. McKay, 1971.

Shea, T.M.: *Teaching Children and Youth with Behavior Disorders*. St. Louis, Mosby, 1978.

Stephens, T.M., Hartman, A.C., and Lucas, V.: *Teaching Children with Basic Skills — A Curriculum Handbook*. Columbus, Merrill, 1978.

Tawney, J.W.: *Programmed Environments Curriculum*. Columbus, Merrill, 1979.

Walker, H.M.: *Walker Problem Behavior Identification Checklist*. Los Angeles, Western Psychological Services, 1976.

Walker, J.E., and Shea, T.M.: *Behavior Modification: A Practical Approach for Educators*. St. Louis, Mosby, 1976.

Wood, M.M.: *Developmental Therapy*. Baltimore, University Park Press, 1975.

INDEX